W9-AQN-732

LAW AND CONSCIENCE

LAW AND CONSCIENCE

BY FRANZ BÖCKLE

translated by M. James Donnelly

SHEED AND WARD : NEW YORK

Nihil Obstat
W. John Fradet
Censor Deputatus
April 20, 1966

Imprimatur
Robert F. Joyce
Bishop of Burlington
April 20, 1966

Law and Conscience *was first published in German, under the title* Gesetz und Gewissen, *by Räber-Verlag, Luzern and Stuttgart.*

Library of Congress Catalog Card Number: 66–22009

Manufactured in the United States of America

PREFACE

THE FOLLOWING ESSAYS are a copy of four lectures delivered by the author in Basle during the spring of 1963 on behalf of the Society for Christian Culture. Present-day Protestant writers on evangelical theological ethics had raised certain questions for Catholic moral theology. These lectures were a first attempt at presenting such questions to a highly interested Catholic audience and at seeking for a personal answer to these problems. At the time, the lectures aroused much attention and certain critics expressed the wish that the lectures be presented in written form to allow more time for reflecting on them. In accord with these suggestions, we here offer to the public the same lectures in a form essentially unchanged. The reader will at once observe that more questions are raised than answered. But the frank baring of mutual problems is well worthwhile.

TRANSLATOR'S ACKNOWLEDGMENT

The translator wishes to thank L. Housey for her generosity in typing the final copy of this work.

M.J.D.

CONTENTS

ABBREVIATIONS

D	Denzinger, *Enchiridion symbolorum,* Barcelona-Freiburg ^{32}1963
KD	Karl Barth, *Kirchliche Dogmatik,* Zollikon 1932–1955
LThK	*Lexikon für Theologie und Kirche,* Freiburg 1957–1963
RGG^{3}	*Die Religion in Geschichte und Gegenwart,* Tübingen ^{3}1957–1962
WA	Martin Luther, *Werke,* Weimarer Ausgabe
ZEE	*Zeitschrift für Evangelische Ethik,* Gütersloh

LAW AND CONSCIENCE

INTRODUCTION

In the present-day ecumenical dialogue, discussion is strikingly faint and insignificant when the subject of ethics is brought up. During the last few years, while engaged in inter-confessional discussions, we have experienced interesting changes: fundamental questions were broached, such as the problem of the forms of thought (H. U. von Balthasar in his explanation of the theology of Karl Barth), or the relationship of Scripture and tradition (J. R. Geiselmann). Crucial differences of doctrine were discussed, such as the teaching on justification by H. Küng, anthropology by H. Volk, ecclesiology by K. Rahner, J. Ratzinger, and others.

Discussion on Christian ethics remained mute, so to speak. From our daily living together, we know that we are engaged in many practical questions of the moral life. The principal foundations of conduct, demanded of the believer by the New Testament, are preached and striven for in all the Churches. But in general, it is also well known that the Catholic receives very detailed moral instruction from his Church. It is not by chance that the impression prevails that Protestants are clearly freer in their form of life. The Catholic is not only bound by ecclesiastical prescriptions (the so-called commandments of the Church), but the Church, through her official interpretation of the claims of the natural law, imposes upon her subjects obligatory instructions, even in very concrete, individual questions. Religious teachers try to make this cramping state of affairs more palatable by the "consoling" suggestion: "Life is easier for a Protestant, but death for a Catholic." "Life is easier for a Protestant!" In back of this statement lies a deep misunderstanding of the Protestant ethics of faith with its central concept of Christian freedom. Life is easier for a Protestant means something like this: Protestants do not have to attend service every Sunday, they have no prescribed days of fast, and they are not obliged under sin to make their Easter duties. And, further: Protestants are also freer with regard to their marriages. If a married relationship has gone on the rocks, they can, after a divorce, eventually remarry. And, if in conscience they feel bound not to have any more children, their Church leaves them a free hand with regard to the selection of methods. This is truly reason enough for speaking about greater freedom in the Protestant Church.

Yet, as already said, it is easier to die as a Catholic. Just once ask a doctor who has had some experience or a nurse with many years of hospital work, whether a death can be classified easier or harder according to the Church in which the dying person was baptized! These examples will not decide the question for us.

The matter goes far deeper than a question of permission or the lack of it. Protestant freedom is not licentiousness and personal obedience in faith to an individual call is not subjectivism, just as binding teaching by the ecclesiastical authority is not a foundation of legalism. The problems go deeper and the differences are much more nuanced. We have to get clear on the meaning of moral norms in the light of the gospel. Does the New Covenant recognize any moral laws at all that are universally binding? If so, what function do they have, then? Such are the fundamental questions. And the different confessions place a different emphasis on their answer to them. Consequently, discussion on ecumenical questions must, above all, consider this fundamental problem.

Protestant theology has developed its ethics as a consequence of its teaching on justification. From this starting point, a strong defense is made against every form of legalizing. Above all, there are two dangers by which they think Catholic theology is threatened. They fear that the Catholic teaching on the moral law could induce man to seek, by means of the fulfillment of the law, to construct a claim to salvation. Accordingly, in the first chapter, we shall examine closely the essence and *function* of law in the New Covenant. Protestant ethics gives a further warning against all too hastily assuming that we can encompass the will of God adequately in propositions and then casuistically apply them to individual cases. According to the conviction of Protestants, the so-called natural moral law must be most carefully considered within the context of theological ethics, if it is not to be completely rejected. The divine command, the invitation extended to an individual Christian, is so concrete in its content, that it can not be deduced from general propositions. In the second and third chapters, we shall consider this *Problematik,* when we examine the validity of the order of creation within the context of the order of grace and when we explain the relationship between norm and situation. Sin will be the subject of the last section and, above all else, we shall try to set limits for the dogmatic and moralistic conceptions of sin.

CHAPTER 1

LAW AND GOSPEL

In this first chapter the question will be made clear whether and in what form, even in the New Covenant, the demands of the Law are to be proclaimed. "Law" (*nomos*) signifies in the New Testament (with a few places excepted) the Mosaic Law. In accord with the late Judaic use of language, at least, the Law not infrequently stands as a part for the whole. It indicates then the whole Sacred Scripture of the Old Testament, viewed as a form of conduct (especially in the combination "Law and Prophets," compare Mt. 7:12; 11:13; 22:40; [5:17]). According to its *content,* the Law signifies the will of God. In the Jewish consciousness, it stands as the living will of God lying behind the written Torah. Indeed, even the teaching of Jesus is nothing else than the proclaiming of this will of God. Therein lies the continuity between the Old and the New Covenant. The will of God forms the actual prevailing content of the Mosaic Law, the Sermon on the Mount, and the apostolic preaching, and even the law written in the heart of the Gentiles (Rom 2:14f.), aims at making this will known.

We are interested here not with this content side of the Law, but rather with its *function* in salvation-history. By function we mean a definite order of relationship in which the will of God draws near to man to become realized in him. In the teaching on the "use of law" (*usus legis*) in Lutheran theology, this function of law plays a very important role.

Before all else, the correct differentiation and relationship between Law and Gospel is crucial. Luther looked upon it as the heart of the Christian message. It is just as fundamental for the proper understanding of justification as for the ethics following therefrom. Hence, Luther calls the distinction between Law and Gospel a "very high, the highest art in Christendom."[1] The sharp alternative is this: Religion of law, or religion of grace! Under this aspect, "Luther very emphatically placed this theme in the middle of all theological thought."[2] For Luther, Law and Gospel are two forms of the Word of God, which do not express the same thing and, yet, belong together. They can neither be separated, nor confused into pell-mell indistinctness. Rather, they must, each in its own way, exercise their finality. In this way, the Law has the first, the Gospel the last word. The Law makes menacing demands, the Gospel confers grace. The result of all this is that by the demand of the Law, man truly dies, so that in Christ fulfillment and life can be given to him. "The way along which the Word leads us looked to him (Luther) like a change in the exactly opposite direction. 'God leads down into hell and back again'—that is

Law and Gospel. For Luther, everything lying in between is in the sphere not of truth, but of illusion."[3] "Thus, the preaching of the Law reveals the nature of lost man. And, as preaching of the Word, therefore, in the embracing of the Gospel through the preaching, it leads to the 'second' use of the Law, a use made legitimate only as coming from justification: '*Evangelium facit ex lege paedagogum in Christum*' (The Gospel makes of the law that which leads on to Christ)."[4] With that it may be clear that, with the classical formulation of the theme "Law and Gospel," we have to deal, primarily, with a theologico-historical and not with an immediately biblical presentation of the question. Besides, in the case of Luther, the distinction has a polemical orientation "both as a defence against the Scholastic legalizing of the Gospel based on the concept of Christ the Lawmaker and against those enthusiasts and their turning of the Gospel into a spiritualized law."[5] Today we are more conscious than ever how polemical statements must be interpreted with careful consideration. In our investigation, this holds true no less, also, for the interpretation of the Pauline doctrine of the Law, in which Luther's distinction has its biblical foundation.

Paul, also, indulges in polemics, inasmuch as he inveighs against the Judaic and rabbinical misunderstanding, according to which Israel has preserved in the Law a means of justification by which Israelites were distinguished from and raised above all other nations. This is a conception that does not correspond to the genuine understanding of Old

Testament Law. Rather it was only in the last parts of the Old Testament that the way was prepared for this conception and it then, especially, came into view in the post-canonical rabbinical literature.* In opposition to this, Paul reveals the salvation-history meaning of the Law hidden up to that time. Namely, the Law has a go-between character (Gal 3:19; Rom 5:30). It is an accessory factor in relation to the promise which is the foundation of salvation and salvation history.[6] Hence, the promise is not dependent upon the fulfilling of the Law, but is bestowed only on account of faith (Gal 3:18; Rom 4:13). The Law has rather the salvation-history destiny to bring the Fall to completion (Rom 5:20), to allow sins to become actual and intensive (Rom 7:7ff.), to make them sensibly manifest (Rom 7:13), and to draw them out in their sinfulness. In this sense the Law is "the power of sin" (1 Cor 15:56), and enables the

* Compare R. Bring, "Die Erfüllung des Gesetzes durch Christus" Old Testament. Compare M. Noth, *Gesammelte Studien zum AT*, München, 1957. "The Law in the Old Testament is not an absolute quantitative whole, so that obedience to the Law entails corresponding reward and punishment. The tendency thus to envisage it was prepared only in the last parts of the Old Testament and then, especially, came into view in the post-canonical rabbinical literature. This means a departure from the former, genuine foundation of faith and life and can not be taken for a factual and correct common conception of the Old Testament nor can it be the basis of a correct presentation of most of the Old Testament laws." In the future, the definition of the Law as a commanding of actions for which there is corresponding reward and punishment must be critically complemented.

sin to become an actual sin. "The Law's role is to perform the deadly, yet, in the end, merciful service of causing sin and death to develop and be revealed unto deeds of death."[7] Thereby, the door is closed on every attempt to establish the Law as something absolute and to use, or rather to abuse, it as a means of self-justification before God.

But it may be asked whether this role of the Law as accuser and judge (one that stands forth prominently in St. Paul judging from the polemic just described) is also the only salvation-history function of the Law. Or, besides this misuse of the Law for self-justification (namely, for hubris, for sin, in opposition to which the Law necessarily assumes the role of tribunal), was there not also, during the time of the Promise, and is there not still even in the New Testament under new signs, a right use of the Law? Was not that also a genuine function of the Law, that relationship of union of the people with their God, a relationship decreed by God in grace to be preserved to the end of time? Therefore, the function of the Law is not only the leading of man into sin, but, also, through the guidance of God's grace, the keeping of man from a sinful fall. Under the grace of God, was there not in the Old Covenant also genuine obedience to the Law? In its biblical function is the scope of the Law adequately described, if looked upon as a court of justice, as a putting external pressure upon man, demanding from him due conduct, and thereby regulating his actions, setting up a discernible relationship between activity and reward, works and salvation, and, hence, establishing moral conduct under an egotistical finality?[8] Then, admittedly, the Law can lead man *only* into sin.

In this view, the setting up of the Law within the framework of the Gospel is all the more out of the question. How then are those moral imperatives founded in the Gospel going to be explained? That, precisely, will be the object of our attention in the following section. It is the key question of Christian ethics. Since Karl Barth wrote *Evangelium und Gesetz* (Gospel and Law),[9] there has been renewed a vigorous discussion of this question in Protestant writings. Actually, within Protestant circles, it has become "the main point of theological controversy."[10] We do not mean to get involved in this dispute among Protestants. Our concern is rather the presentation of the Protestant concern, given especially clear expression in the controversy. And then, above all, we shall deal with the question of the extent to which this concern belongs likewise to and is understood in Catholic moral theology.

THE CONCERN OF THE REFORMERS*

The theology of the Reformers bases every attempt to found a system of Christian ethics on the fundamental dogma of Christ as *the unique Mediator* of salvation. There-

* Since in theological ethics the difference between the Reformed and Lutheran tradition is rightly pointed out clearly, we distinguish the two concepts where such a distinction is called for. As a common conception for both traditions we use the expression, "Ethics of the Reformers."

fore, the Law and its fulfillment may never, not even in its loftiest form, become a mediator of salvation. Hence, the fundamental position of the Reformation—justification only from grace in faith in Christ—is also made the basic tenet of all evangelical ethics.[11]

In spite of this, the Law has for the Christian and his moral life a real meaning and, consequently, must be continually proclaimed to the Christian community. This has "since Luther's death, never been questioned in evangelical ethics."[12] In view of this, it is crucial that its function be not misunderstood and the Gospel's message of grace be not weakened. Granted that our view is correct, the common evangelical position of the Lutheran and reformed position can be included in three assertions:

1. *The Gospel as the message of redemption by Christ destroys every form of human self-justification.* The extent of harmony in the present discussion rests "on this, that the opposition of Law and Gospel is meaningful and necessary, provided that thereby is meant the opposition of religion by Law and life from faith in the Gospel."[13] Religion by Law is had when a man understands the commandments and, indeed, the actual commandments of God (even that of love), as a demand imposed upon him to achieve, "by his own power, religious and moral activity and, by means of this conduct, to make certain for himself a claim to the good pleasure of God and, above all, a moral self-assurance in preference to all the 'Godless.' "[14] This would be that misuse

of the Law of God which Jesus condemned in the Pharisees (Lk 18:1–14), and against which Paul inveighed. This is the "great betrayal which sin effects by means of the Law."[15]

The Gospel is diametrically opposed to such a religion by Law. It says that no man can by his own activity take his stand before God. The Gospel is a pure word of grace even where (as with Karl Barth) it takes on the form of the Law. That would be precisely "our actual sin, that we 'in seeking justification through the Law' (Rom 9:31) would pay no attention to the Gospel in the Law and not want to have Christ hold good as the goal of the Law."[16] In the Gospel God portrays Himself as one who out of free grace pardons the sinner and gives him life. And we have it revealed to us that we have in no wise either the power or the right to live except through His grace. Thus the Gospel is "an invitation to abandon religion by law with its desire to make self the foundation of religion, and to come on to the life of faith which is the clinging to Christ present. And, finally, the Gospel calls man to the renunciation, in Christ, of his desire for independence and urges self-surrender to grace and love of God, which alone can give us a foundation and support."[17] In this sense, as announcement and acceptance of that which I am out of pure grace, the Gospel puts an end to the Law as a demanding action for justification.

2. *The Gospel does not take away the will of God, but directly preaches of its fulfillment through Christ and our*

sharing in it. According to His own words, Christ did not come to take away the Law, but to fulfill it (Mt 5:17). As far as the content of the Law goes, it proclaims the will of God "and, indeed, not a transient but His actual permanent will."* And Christ has revealed and at the same time fulfilled this holy will of God in its mysterious depths. "In Christ the Law comes into contact with us in a clearer form, as a law fulfilled and consummated."[18] That is the real meaning of Romans 10:4, according to which Christ is the goal, the summit, and fulfillment of the Law. "For Paul, this signifies that Christ stands for the whole of the Old Testament truth and that not, indeed, simply as a repetition or imitation of this truth, but as its fulfillment in word and deed."[19] Hence, the validity of the will of God also in the New Testament is not taken away. "It would be a wrong interpretation of Luther, were one to accept as his the view that the Old Testament and the Law were abrogated by Christ. This opinion had been held by Marcion and, again, towards the turn of the century, was common among circles of liberal theologians. . . ."** Thus, as the

* J. Gollwitzer, *Zur Einheit von Gesetz und Evangelium,* Antwort, Zürich, 1956, 292. Compare W. Joest, *Gesetz und Freiheit,* 29: His opinion is that, with Luther, also, continuity prevails in the question of content. "Here the wish of the Law forms one with what the Gospel effects."

** R. Bring, *op. cit.,* 10. Compare K. Barth, *Evangelium und Gesetz* (*Gospel and Law*), II: "Therefore, with extreme earnestness, Paul calls the Law holy and its precepts holy, right, and good (Rom 7:12). He protests against it, because it may be contrary to the Promise (Gal 3:21).

Gospel testifies, God does not waive the fulfillment of those things mentioned in the content of the Law. By personal works, to be sure, man cannot fulfill the Law; but through Christ and united in faith with Him, we are His associates in the fulfilling of the Law. The Law fulfilled by Christ may now "be fulfilled by the believer in his role as a new man. This fulfillment is, so to speak, an aftereffect, a consequence of man's own existence which is already latent in the fulfilling of the Law.*

3. *Insofar as the Gospel does lay down demands, these do not mean demands for action that we must accomplish as leading to our salvation; but rather the Gospel demands are a counsel pointing out things we may venture to achieve as a fruit of our salvation.* No one denies that the Gospel contains a full measure of instructions for the Christian life and we have already become acquainted with how the content of these demands is continuous with the Mosaic Law. But, do these demands just extend the role of the Law

---

He says that it has much rather been given us for an increase of life (Rom 7:10). He explains (in harmony with the well-known words of the Sermon on the Mount [Mt 5:17f.]), that the preaching of faith does not mean the taking away, but the establishment of the Law (Rom 3:21). Paul presents himself as the Apostle of the Gentiles, as ἔννομος Χριστοῦ (as one standing in the law of Christ) (1 Cor 9:21)."

* W. Joest, *Gesetz und Freiheit,* 126, with reference to E. Seeberg, *Luthers Theologier,* Göttingen, 1929–1937, II, 113, according to which the saints participate in the fulfillment of the law of Christ.

as a juridical sanction, insofar as the Christian is just another man and sinner? Or do these instructions manifest a new, the so-called third, use of the Law? While the Reformers with Calvin labeled this third use of the Law as the most important (*praecipuus usus legis*), the expression, at least, will not please Lutherans,[20] although actually it seems to have been known to Luther[21] and is admitted by many Lutherans today. Some understand the prescriptions of the New Testament as a genuine function of the Law.[22] These same New Testament precepts are explained by others as an "office of the Law," *usus practicus evangelii* (Joest), as a "counsel" (Schlink), or as a "commandment" (Althaus). Whatever may be the case, all are at one in maintaining that obedience to these instructions may not be reckoned as a condition for salvation. The commandments are helps for the preservation, strengthening, and increasing justification through faith.

Besides this passing over (*transitus*) from the state of sin to that of justification, there is also the matter of going forward (*progressus*). "It is possible, from day to day, to become holier and better. This holds good, indeed, in such a way that the heart, eyes, hands, tongue, and feet are now actually engaged otherwise than before."[23] Viewed thus, works are required for the maintenance and increase of faith and the New Testament precepts appear as a guidepost to such a practice of works that maintain and strengthen faith.

> Our Christian state, seen as coming from God to us, is at every moment a gift rendered, and, at the same time, at every moment, seen as from and for us, is a gift surrendered. To the extent that God gives it to us, we may and must look upon our Christian being as a *state of being,* that now becomes effective and in virtue of the power of love of God brings forth 'fruit.' But although faith and the new life, in that it comes to us from God, is a true state of being, still, what is on our side is actually real no other than being called daily to activity proper to this new state of life: acts of faith and love.[24]

This state of being, therefore, has its reality only in personal activity. It may never be looked upon as a permanent state of being. To this extent Althaus goes along with Thielicke, but he does not limit the Gospel command, as does Thielicke, (as it were) releasing the clutch on faith and thereby setting into gear (so to speak) a powerful form of moral automatic action.*

* Compare H. Thielicke, *Theologische Ethik* I, 316–365. Thielicke holds fast to a clear line of demarcation between Law and Gospel. According to him, the depths of the existential situation of man before God can be properly grasped only if it is seen under the fundamentally indissoluble tension between Law and Gospel. The fundamental indissolubility of this tension rests thereon, that the union lying in back of and "taking away" this tension is not known. The close union of God the Judge and

That would be a distortion of the picture of the fruit. It can only manifest that essential necessity, by which the gospel apprehended in faith urges man to the act of love. This necessity, however, is not automatically effectual, but only by way of personal decisions and actions of man. As Christians we also stand fixed under the "ought to" and the "must" (counsel and obligation), of which the Augustana speaks, therefore, under the precept that lies enclosed in the offering of the Gospel. The Christian life maintains the character of an obedience, of a constantly fresh decision for that holy movement, which flowing from the embracing love of God, holds us fast and impels us to love in act.[25]

THE CATHOLIC ANSWER

In order to go back and grasp the great Catholic tradition in the way that it again today is taking on a strong living form, we must disregard the textbooks of the last three cen-

---

the man given grace—this is visible. If we try to bring out a teleological relationship between Law and Gospel, between sanctimoniousness and the love of God, then we weaken both of them: "The *Law* is robbed of its nature, in that it no longer brings along the *whole* tribunal of justice; one no longer encounters death in it. *Grace* is thereby deprived of strength, in that it no longer raises us from the dead, since we are not dead at all" (*Theologie der Anfechtung,* 1949, 83).

turies, books over-freighted with canon law. The narrowness and overemphasis of the formulated law was partially "anti-Protestantism." And, partially, it has its motivating power in the modern scientific ideal that in the science of nature was wholly devoted to law."[26] G. Söhngen has performed an undeniable service in bringing anew to the attention of present-day theology the Catholic theological tradition of the theme of Law and Gospel.[27]

The *point of departure* lies *in the Pauline doctrine of law,* not only in the law of demands and sanctions which was superseded by the grace of the Gospel, but in the equally Pauline teaching of the "Law of Christ" (Gal 6:2), of the "Law of the Spirit of the life in Christ Jesus" (Rom 8:2). This is the law "that Christ himself fulfilled for our benefit and which speaks to men who are fundamentally renewed through this fulfilling."[28] The attitude of the Apostle Paul towards the Mosaic Law is defined essentially through his position as missionary to the Gentiles. His struggle for the Gentiles' freedom from observing the Mosaic Law was, above all, a struggle against the absolute necessity of the Law for salvation. In opposition to this, Paul will vehemently point out that not the law, but Christ alone and membership in the Israel renewed in Christ is, for all men and for all times, the only way of salvation. In Christ's substitute death for our sins, God has revealed His own righteousness and the righteousness of men included therein (compare Rom 3:21–26). All human righteousness is one, coming purely from grace and faith; this is the only way to obtain it. Paul repeats continually his thesis around this point, that no man by reason of the works of the law becomes the seed of Abraham and thereby justified, but only through faith (Rom 3:20, 28; Gal 2:16, 21; 3:11). Paul shows even from Scripture itself the powerlessness of the Law, past or present, ever to be a way of salvation. The thesis that no man can be saved other than through faith is really a Scriptural citation (Ps 143:2, completed in accord with the meaning of "through works of the Law"). The example of Abraham (Rom 3:31–4:25; Gal 3:6–9) shows with special clearness that, according to Scripture (Gen 15:6), the Law never was, nor was it meant to be a way [to justification], but that righteousness is given to men only by reason of faith and as a purely unmerited grace of God. Anyone explaining the Law with its demand for actions and the corresponding fulfillment of works as a means for salvation has misunderstood the Law. Against such a false explanation Paul can but protest. To that end he now reveals the salvation-history meaning of the Law hidden up to that time, namely, the Law has a go-between character. It stands at the service of the promise. This, however, is not dependent upon the fulfilling of the Law (God had surely given the promise to Abraham long before the proclamation of the Law). The promise was given only on the ground of faith (Gal 3:18; Rom 4:13). The efficacy of the Law has rather always consisted in this that it makes man in sin experience his need for redemption. The Law, indeed, as such, can never give man the power to do the good that it demands. On the contrary, when it meets with unredeemed man, it leads him on to the breaking of the Law. In this sense, the Law is the "power of sin" (1 Cor 15:56).

In the *Introduction* we have already indicated that this was not the only salvation-history meaning of the Law. But, in his struggle against every legalistic abuse of the Law, Paul was at that time especially forced to explain the Mosaic Law in this salvation-history function of teacher as henceforth having been victoriously superseded by Christ. By that Paul does not want to free man saved only through grace from moral obligation. The Christian must place himself freely and completely at the service of God to whom he belongs through baptism (Rom 6). Through the Spirit given him, he ought to mortify the works of the body (the unredeemed man, Rom 8:13). He ought also to walk in the Spirit, in whom he lives (Gal 5:25). Now Paul ventures in a new meaning to speak even further of the Law. The one living under the grace of Christ is no outlaw, even though he does not stand "under the Law" (Rom 6:15), neither under the Law of Moses, nor under any law at all considered simply as an external force. He is much rather one "living in the law of Christ" (1 Cor 9:21). In dying, Christ fulfilled the Law and thus became for us source of the divine *Pneuma.* This *Pneuma,* the Holy Spirit given to us, is the new law, the "law of Christ" (Gal 6:2). As the supernatural power of God, this Law changes us within and gives the power to fulfill the will of God (Rom 8:3).

> The Apostle demands, therefore, that God's will be done. But with the Christian this fulfillment takes place differently (in a different way) than in the old Law. He does not have to listen to a host of commands coming to him from without and with which he cannot comply. Instead, from within he hearkens to the voice of the Spirit which at the same time urges him on to and empowers him for doing good. Thus the "law of the Spirit" is not a new codex of law, but rather an urging going out from the Holy Spirit towards good.[29]

However, this "Law of the Spirit" should not be pictured simply as an inner encouragement from the Holy Spirit. This is so because its fulfillment in love that looks back to the preaching of the great commandment by Jesus and Paul also makes special reference to the instructions of Jesus (compare 1 Cor 7:10, 25; 9:14; 14:37). The present state of the newly acquired existence in Christ is insistent in its urging to action, to the formation of the life in Christ.

A glance at theological reflection shows us a happy agreement with biblical teaching.

St. Augustine, in his late writing, *De spiritu et littera* (On the Spirit and the Letter), expounded this theme both under the aspect of opposition and that of relationship of union between law and grace (free will and election). The opposition, on the one side, lies between the "external placing" and carrying out of the letter and, on the other side, the "inner giving" of the Holy Spirit for fulfilling the spirit of the law in love. "There on Sinai the finger of God wrote on stone tablets, here in the hearts of men with the sending of the Spirit and Pentecost. On Sinai, therefore, the Law, with which the unrighteous would be made righteous, was set up from without (*extrinsecus posita*)."[30] Augustine expresses the analogy of the law in the salvation-history association of the relation of Law and grace to the relation of Promise and fulfillment: "The Law was given, so that the (promised) grace might be sought after; grace was given, that the Law might be fulfilled."[31] The means by which the Law lays bare the "prudence" of the "flesh" is the way this "prudence" uses the Law. Christ fulfilled the Law. In the communion of life with Him (grace), the fulfilling of the Law becomes possible for us in such wise that our merits (*merita*) really are but the gifts (*munera*) of God. In place of the *fac quod iubeo* ("do what I order") of the Law, there comes the *da quod iubes* ("give what you order") of faith. Thereby the law of love comes into prominence and every instance of movement towards salvation is attributed exclusively to grace (XIII, 22).

Thomas Aquinas, in connection with Paul and Augustine, develops his teaching of the law of the Gospel in the *Summa Theologica* (I-II qq. 106–108). He answers with a meaningful distinction the first question, whether the law of the Gospel is a written law (q. 106, a.1). The most important thing in the New Testament, that which makes up its whole strength (*in quo tota virtus euis consistit*), is not written down as in the Old Testament, but inscribed in the hearts of men. And that is the grace of the Holy Spirit which is conferred through faith in Christ. For this Thomas refers expressly to Paul (Rom 3:27; 8:2), and to Augustine (*De spiritu et littera*). And, as a consequence, he says in the following article that this grace (and presence) of the Holy Spirit given interiorly makes man righteous. And then, following Augustine almost verbatim: "There, namely in the Old Covenant, the Law was established to frighten the unrighteous. Here, namely in the New Covenant, there was given a law interiorly such as to make man righteous."

Besides this chief point there is another which pertains, only in second place, to the law of the New Covenant. This is the written law, the gospel as a documentary ordinance. Thomas has in mind here (compare q. 108, a.2) the institution of the sacraments, the biblical command to love, and the Decalogue. As statutes they are, vis-à-vis grace, entirely of the second rank. For that reason, as precepts existing outside man, they could not make him righteous. That is why the letter of the gospel, also, would bring death, were the saving grace of faith not bestowed interiorly.

Thomas sees, therefore, the role of the written law wholly from the viewpoint of interior grace. The relation is twofold: first, Thomas speaks of *dispositions for grace* (*quaedam sicut dispositiva ad gratiam*). Although he follows Augustine here, we may recognize therein the accusing function (*usus elenchticus*) of the Law, especially inasmuch as the Law expressed in negative form constantly warns man of his sins, convinces him of sin, and thus causes grace continually to be sought anew and gratefully experienced.

In the second place he speaks of the *right use of grace* (*quaedam ad usum huius gratiae*). Grace urges man on to fruitful works. And the positive instructions of the gospel, in particular, bolster up this prompting of grace and give it direction. They never, however, prescribe things which we of ourselves must achieve for our salvation, but suggest and indicate actions which we may effect as a result of our actual sanctification.

> Thomas, therefore, preceives a law in the gospel, but, for him, the "newness" of the gospel law does not lie in the legal character of this law, but in something not having the nature of a law. This "law" consists in grace, faith, and the presence of the Holy Spirit, they themselves in no way having the character of a law. This would then be a law purely in an analogous and relative sense.[32]

Therewith follows an all-emphatic statement that the law of the gospel may not be looked upon as a collection of external prescriptions. And a Christian would greatly err, were he to wish for himself exclusively "legalistic" guidance in the guise of an external, negative, universal law, and, perhaps, even in opposition to the inner guidance of grace, might wish to keep himself free for a call towards the inconstancy of a general law.

If we now take this teaching of the great Catholic tradition together with a look at the Council of Trent, we can offer the following as an answer to the concern of the Protestants:

1. Even if it is portrayed as analogous to a law, the gospel still stands in sharp contrast to every attempt to use any law whatsoever as a means for justification before God. In the first chapter of the decree on justification, the Council of Trent expressly declares that nature and the Mosaic Law are completely incapable of justifying man (D 793). And, with respect to the New Testament, we have heard St. Thomas say that, without prevenient grace, its written prescriptions are a dead letter. Objectively, justification, as the gracious judicial pronouncement of God in Jesus Christ, is God's work alone. Subjectively, of course, in sanctification it is necessary that man, in his passivity, be active in the highest degree: he must submit himself in faith to the divine decision. This means man must, because of the righteousness of God revealed in His law, allow himself to stand convicted of his sins and be shaken with holy fear, and

then he must trustingly embrace God's word of forgiveness. In this "cooperation" on the part of man, there is not a question of a co-production of an effect, but rather of an "association on man's part in that which has been put into operation by God alone."[33]

2. The Law is not taken away for the person made righteous in Christ, but is brought to real status.

> Christ is not the "end" of the Law in this sense that God's demand and its fulfillment cease to be. He is the "end" of the Law rather in this way, namely, that the law of the Jews and Gentiles, the law of the world, thereby in Him come to an end in that He himself now sets up *His* law. The law of God, dealing with both body and soul, simply is heard anew.[34]

That is the meaning of the Council of Trent when, in speaking of Christ the Lawmaker (D 831), it says that Christian freedom would be misunderstood, were it preached as freedom from the observance of the commandments (D 804). The teachings of the gospel make up a unity with the new, inner law (*usus practicus evangelii*), and do not exist simply outside the law of grace of the Holy Spirit or as an addition to it. "From the side of the interior law of charity, the external law is not a simple boundary line, but rather a living enclosure which, with the increase of charity, reveals itself ever more clearly in its inner dynamism that tends towards the golden heart of love."[35]

> This is the prerequisite of the gospel, Pauline, and Joannine ethics; it rules over all and is a foundation for everything. The oneness of what we are and what we ought to be is not something to be attained by our own efforts, but that which has already been made a reality in God and in which we share by grace. And this oneness must unquestionably be realized in us. This "must" (*dieses Mussen*), because it is based on divine necessity, exercises the most absolute demand on the entire man, his every effort, his entire station in life, his entire being.[36]

But since the redeemed man is also a sinner,

> the Law expressed in prohibitive form, the restrictive barrier of the Law written on tablets, continues in force as an indictment and unmasking of the carnal man. Even more, in unity with the law of the Spirit inscribed in the heart through baptism, the restrictive law can now even more sharply indict the sinner. The external Law continues necessary as a training ground for the properly interior Law, because it makes known and reveals the bringer of death, the *sarx* (flesh) and the *hamartia* (sin).[37]

3. *The fruitfulness of the Christian life in obedience to the law means no reestablishment of the Law as a principle of conduct.*

> Where Christ is preached as lawgiver and the gospel as new law, Luther suspected that, under the pretext of the Cross, which throughout the gospel was the source of every demand and all activity, man's claims and activity would yet have the last word. Therein persists the danger that God be robbed of being the one and only good, the sole cause and giver, and that man be robbed of confidence for venturing to renounce all that he owns before God.[38]

In line with the right understanding of the Council of Trent,* we would rather say with Hans Küng: here "holds good the fact that God causes everything, but from God's causing everything it does not follow that God alone produces all that He causes, but—and this is the most beautiful marvel of God's being the cause of all things—man's co-causality flows from God's causality."[39] In principle, this holds good likewise for man's cooperation with regard to justification, such as in the case of subjective, moral

* Trent forbade holding that the gospel, without the *conditio* of the observance of the commandments, was the bare and unconditioned promise of eternal life (D 830). The *conditio* is a *removens prohibens* that can be taken over by the grace of the Holy Spirit.

sanctification in obedient love that follows consequent upon justification. Everything comes from God, even man's co-operation. The righteousness given to man through justification by God is the basis for every moral sanctification of man.

> Without the divinely-given holiness, man's sanctifying himself is worthless—for the former is the foundation of the latter; and God-given holiness is unfruitful without man's sanctifying himself through grace. In all human sanctification, it is evident that there is no question of a completion of that which is human, but only of an effect of divine activity.[40]

If the man living in faith consummates what he has begun, then

> there is not really a striving towards perfection from man's side, but a radiation of the same from God. This takes place not in view of the distinction between what man is and what he should be, but it proceeds from the absolute knowledge and requirement that the divine oneness of what is and what ought to be, which lives in man through grace, must endure always in man's life.[41]

Does this not strike a harmonious chord with the thesis of W. Joest? Namely, "In accord with the New Testament,

Luther understands sanctification not as a human process going forth towards the divine decree of salvation, but as a movement towards us of this salvation-decree—and all this in the resurrection of Jesus Christ, the fundamental cause of the new creature's entering into our earthly reality." Truly, justification and sanctification belong together as *one* gift of the gospel.

This is our reply to the question of the meaning of the Law in the gospel.

CHAPTER 2

PRECEPT AND ORDER OF NATURE

So FAR, we have raised the question whether, in order to be true to its promise, the Law given by God through Moses to the people of Israel was to be abrogated in the New Covenant or was to continue valid under the gospel of Christ. We replied that Christ did not come to take away the Law, but to fulfill it. The Law contains the will of God. Christ himself fulfilled this will even to the surrender of his life. He has called and enabled us, following in His lead, to share in this fulfillment. We are in no way exempted from obedience to the will of God as it comes to be expressed in the Law. We are subject to obedience and a court of justice. But we dare not abuse the law in seeking, by our own powers, to perform religious and moral activities in order by these actions to assure ourselves of a claim to God's good pleasure. In this sense, neither for Abraham, nor for Luther, nor for Trent, is there question of justification through the works of the Law. Being called and sanctified are and remain the work of the grace of God. Thereby is thrown out the first accusation of an ultra-legalizing in the sense of a more or less sublime self-redemption on the part of man. We are and became justified only on the basis of faith. The will of God, however, must without restriction be preached to the one called in faith, that he may live, bring forth fruit, and be open for conversion which never comes to an end.

The will of God, therefore, is to be preached. And this gives rise to a second, twofold question: whence comes recognition of God's will and how is this communicated to man? With regard to the sources of this knowledge, there prevails, before all else, an important controversy in reference to the so-called law of nature. It is especially the question of the validity of the order of nature within the order of grace. In a first section (I.), we shall take up this question. In a second (II.), we shall have to ask ourselves whether and how the concrete will of God is to be apprehended in general laws.

I. THE VALIDITY OF THE ORDER OF CREATION

Among the fundamental problems in the history of jurisprudence must be ranked the relationship of power and law. Again and again, and most especially in times of human crises, this has lead to great tensions and corresponding disputes between theories of the state based upon the absolutist and natural-law theories.

Within the Protestant ethics of the present, the public

abuse of power by the totalitarian state in the post-war era has led to new reflection upon a particular tradition, that of the natural law.* Leading the way for all was Emil Brunner, who, with his doctrine of the order or creation and righteousness, latched onto the western law-of-nature tradition. He consciously understands his thinking as a reaction against the positivistic theory of law and against theories putting

* The multiplicity of terminology demands, first of all, a clearing up of concepts. In connection with the doctrine on the law of nature we run up against the concepts: natural moral law, moral law of nature, right of nature, natural right. These concepts are used with a partly synonymous, and partly a clearly differentiated content. With regard to content, they are distinguished thus:

1. The first principle of moral consciousness (primitive or original conscience, synderesis: The principle perceptible to every man: "To do good and avoid evil!").

2. The moral law which is independent of every positive law and is developed, with the help of intelligent reason (*ratio*). Often defined as the "sum of those moral norms which can be known to man as moral from the nature of things in virtue of his natural understanding.

3. That section of the moral law, which refers to righteousness (justice) in the inter-human relationships and the claims actually contained in them. Here is meant the *right of nature,* that is, the right order existing prior to all positive legislation; the integrating part of the natural moral order, from which the moral order has its absolutely binding power.

4. The legitimate laying claim to a possibility, which gives one an objective right.

So much for the concepts having to do with our questions and their limitation, which, however, are far from always and everywhere being adhered to by authors and the official teaching.

power and law on the same footing. Brunner's efforts to link up the theological precept with the political order in an ecclesial-social activism found agreement among many laymen (Schönfeld, Ellul). His thought, certainly, did not remain free from opposition by critics. From the theological side (the spokesman for all was Karl Barth), Brunner was reproached with a mitigated Thomism, which, if thought out further, would have necessarily led him, in consequence, to the Catholic teaching on the law of nature. *Pro* and *con,* it called forth a very fruitful inner-Protestant effort for a theological foundation of law from the order of God's creation and conservation. At the present time the discussion is still far from being ended, even though rather somewhat abated. At any rate, it provides us with a ready-to-hand means of drawing up a kind of balance sheet.

From the Catholic side, a twofold movement is manifest:

On the one side, in its moral decisions of the last ten years, the ecclesiastical *magisterium* has relied more and strongly upon the natural law. A comparison with the documents of the *magisterium* of earlier centuries would enable one to point out this clearly striking and surprising fact.[1]

On the other side, the theological altercations within present-day Protestant theology, reflection going back to Sacred Scripture as the source of revelation, and the flourishing anew of Patristics have not remained without influence upon the Catholic doctrine on the natural law. With these must be associated the disputes with existentialist thought and its situation ethics. While in the Protestant camp the practical question of *the foundation of law* stood and stands today, before all else, in the foreground and certainly calls forth lively theoretical disputes, the foundation of law does not cause any especially great problems in Catholicism. Here reliance upon a constant tradition is possible. The reason in Catholic thought leading to a new reflection on the foundation of the natural law were rather the renewal of theology from the sources, together with the prospect of dialogue with Protestant theology and the attack of existentialism against a trans-temporal order of being.

From what has been said the limits of the *Problematik* become clear to us. In what follows we do not intend to deal with the question of the foundation of law. There is, then, no question of disputing with juridical positivists nor will there be concern with the question of the so-called "exact law" (*richtigen Recht*). We envisage the subject in a wider and likewise narrower sense: wider, in that we are investigating not only the law of nature (in the strict sense), but also the natural moral law; narrower, inasmuch as we are pushing into the foreground the strictly theological *Problematik*. We have also to deal with an ecumenical problem: does the morality of the New Covenant tolerate the inclusion of, or at least the limiting recourse (Rückgriff) to, a natural moral law? In proportion to our support of this question, a decision is indirectly made about the possibility and meaning of the law of nature in the narrow sense and, thereby, about the foundation of a so-called Christian business-or-state-ethics.

THE PROTESTANT VIEW

Before turning to the individual representatives and their view of the question of the law of nature, we should like to glance here at the fundamental presuppositions of Protestant theology.

A. The Protestant Presuppositions

1. *The teaching of the total corruption of human nature after the Fall:* The doctrine of man as one rooted in sin, as a logical consequence, takes away the theological basis for a natural knowledge of God and morality. To be sure, this did not yet hold good of all the Reformers themselves who still admitted a natural knowledge of God and the good; but the Protestant conception of sin bore within itself a tendency leading to scepticism in the face of every so-called natural theology. The theology of the present day offers us a persuasive example for this development. The divergences in anthropolgy similarly show a consequently different position in the question concerning the law of nature. This is, indeed, shown most clearly in the matter of a general and special revelation (a), and in the question dealing with the connecting-point between the two (b).

a). While individual theologians (Brunner, Althaus),

with rather express appeal to Calvin and Luther, in addition to the special revelation of Scripture (*revelatio specialis*), held to the idea of a universal revelation (*revelatio generalis*), other theologians (especially K. Barth, but also well-known Künneth and Thielicke) refused such a distinction, at least for the time of fallen nature.

Brunner exposes the thought of St. Paul in the *Letter to the Romans,* so that God's revelation, taken objectively, is given in God's creation to every man, and this in itself is enough for a knowledge of God. What is erroneous in natural revelation is not to be sought on the objective plane. The source of error lies exclusively in man's false interpretation of the actual knowledge available to him. It is precisely the fact that God reveals to man clearly and distinctly what is necessary for him to know that is the presupposition of man's actual sin. Even after man's falling into sin, creation did not stop showing forth God's wisdom and divinity. God wants man to learn of Him in creation. That man finds false gods, instead of God, in creation is a product of man's imagination. Scripture teaches that man avoids true knowledge and it is just right there that the real paradox of man lies. In opposition to such a conception, Barth proclaims his radical "No." It is his opinion that, besides the revelation in Scripture, there is no genuine, general revelation of God, either in nature or in man's conscience, and not even in history. There is only *one* revelation and that, indeed, in Christ.

b). From the distinction between the general and special

revelation it follows that *Brunner* must presuppose also for the natural (the "pre-Christian") man a starting point, namely, a capacity for understanding the revelation in Christ. Despite this, Brunner clings to the Protestant doctrine of the corruption of nature (*corruptio naturae*), and he is helped in that by an understanding of grace limited to acts and man's person (*ein rein aktualistisch und personalistisches Verständnis der Gnade*) and linked up with this the distinction into man's being a formal and material image of God (*imago Dei*). Being a formal image consists in responsibility given with reasoning ability; the material, on the contrary, consists in love and union with God. This latter has been completely lost and, precisely on that account, man can, of himself, only continue to misuse his responsibility.

Barth and his school utterly reject every form of connecting-link. Such a conception would be a radical contradiction of the truth that the grace of Christ the Redeemer alone produces effects. Creation can, theologically, only be understood as a presupposition of redemption and hence can only be grasped in faith. The single guarantee of a good world, indestructible in its nature, is Christ, in whom God, before and in the foundation of the world, preserves what exists from destruction.

2. *The teaching of the complementary relation of Law and Gospel:* The Protestant conception of the law of nature —especially in the Lutheran tradition—can not be divorced

from the supplementary relation of Law and Gospel. We have already spoken about this in the first chapter. The end result of our contact with the divine law, whether in the Decalogue, the natural moral law, or in the teaching of the New Testament, is simply to convince us that, with our own moral strivings, we can never fulfill it (*usus elenchticus legis*). The Law is, certainly, a genuine and serious demand of God, but, at the same time, an excessive demand beyond our powers, of which the educational meaning in salvation lies in convincing the sinner of his helplessness to do the will of God. Only on condition of being thus instructed will man become rightly open for hearing the word of God, the glad news, the gospel, saying to him that, in spite of all his sins, he is loved by and pleasing to God. As long as man is a wayfarer on this earth, he must hearken to both words: the word of the Law telling him that, forevermore, he will be a sinner; and, in like manner, the word of the Gospel assuring him that, by looking upon the righteousness of Christ, he may venture to live by his faith. Thus he is *peccator simul et iustus* (a sinner and, at the same time, a righteous man). Insofar as, by grace alone, he now receives the word of redemption, a new obedience is established, not one in reference to a demanding law, but obedience out of grateful love. One so freed from the burden of the Law stands in the "freedom of the Christian man." He is "a free Lord over all things and subject to no one." Freed from all norms, he subjects himself to God simply out of love of other men. With reference to the antithesis between Law and Gospel, Brunner defends the reformed orthodoxy of his teaching on the law of nature against Barth. He says:

> Natural man's self-knowledge from the Law has to come to an end proper to it; and with it the self-sufficient man. Hence, the work of the Law is God's *opus alienum* (a work not God's own). God, as it were, goes after man on his way and leads him right to the end of this way, until he can show the other way, the right way, the way of grace. This is a path that will lead man again to the original being, to existence in the grace-giving word of God. Thus, there is had the series: Law and—then—Gospel.[2]

On that account (this is Brunner's meaning), neither the fact of a natural revelation nor that of the connecting-link must be denied. There has to be brought into question only the quality of these data. In that regard, it is important to maintain that the formal personality, the connecting-point for God's revelation, does not imply any capacity for self-redemption, but, on the contrary, entails the expression of the greatest discontinuity. A natural conscience and natural reason impose upon man a great responsibility. Knowledge bears guilt as a consequence and, for this reason, the natural knowledge of God becomes really a knowledge of the angry

God. Hence, every possibility for self-redemption through man's being a formal image of God, is excluded.

The teaching of the two regimes is most closely connected with the Lutheran antithesis of Law and Gospel. According to Luther's own words there is "a kingdom of two kinds: one is the kingdom of God, the other the kingdom of the world. That of God is a kingdom of grace and mercy, that of the world is a kingdom of anger and severity." The Law is related to the kingdom of the world (kingdom on the left hand of God). The Gospel, the tidings of grace, refers to the kingdom of God (on the right). Both kingdoms and, hence, Law and Gospel are closely interrelated. This distinction of the two kingdoms—seemingly for the first time through the interpretation of Melanchthon—lead to the complete separation of the precept of love and the inner world-order, of the law of the Redeemer and that of God the Conserver, and the distinction of moral theology from natural-law ethics. Throughout the worldly kingdom, God works as creator and conserver; through the spiritual kingdom, God works as redeemer and creator anew. Both regimes exist next to one another, but in no instance should one infringe upon the other. The State should not wish to become the Church and the Church must not venture to become a lawmaker, and neither in the political sphere nor for the spiritual and ecclesial life.[3] This separation is, for the the most part, a source of difficulty for present-day Protestant theology.

B. Protestant Endeavors

The chief stimulus to the present-day discussion about thinking on the natural law derived from Emil Brunner. Brunner, as we already know, took a positive position regarding the idea of a general revelation outside Scripture. He called it an evidently Christian conception.[4] Just as evidently, to be sure, he clung to the belief that this general revelation did not suffice for a knowledge of God such as would lead to salvation. With this in view, he distinguished very clearly between the objective and subjective factor of this knowledge.

Christian thinking on righteousness is based on the order of God's creation.

> A being is right (just) which fits in with the order of the Creator. That is right (just) which God gives to every creature with its essence through the law of this essence and its relation to other creatures. The "primordial order," the point of reference for everything labeled as something 'right' ('just') or 'not right' ('unjust') is the order of creation, behind which stands the will of the Creator.[5]

Hence, nature and the will of God belong together.

For that reason, Christian theologians, also, could make their own this concept of the law of nature (*lex naturae*) and of the right of nature (*ius naturale*). "By the 'law of nature' Christians mean nothing else than the order of creation."[6] Despite their strong insistence on the corruption of human nature, the Reformers also have been able to take over this concept. They did so because they were convinced that the constant element in nature which was called right (just) and "proceeded from the nature of man created by God"[7] was not destroyed through sin. The fact that God, in spite of the sin of man, had kept this order of creation in existence was for them a direct proof of God's goodness. The constants of God's creation are the reason why each one gets what belongs to him. "Reverence for the Creator demands, as the first requirement, submission towards what has been given and a grateful acceptance of the created goods in the various orders."[8]

To be sure, saying that creation is arranged into an order is not the last and only thing to be said in this case. For the clarity of man's understanding (*ratio*) and consequent insight into this order of nature have been disturbed by his sin and the natural order itself has, in many ways, been damaged by sin.

Therefore, for man, who must direct his activity towards the coming Kingdom of God, the testimony given by the order of nature remains indefinite for the glory of God. As long as Brunner wants this giving of testimony to remain inconclusive, because human knowledge, in many instances, is not sufficient and, therefore, appeal is made to the special revelation, we can go along with him on this point. But, with Brunner, the opposition between general and special revelation goes deeper: God's will is not bound up with the order of nature. Law and precept are much rather norms which God, in actual situations, constantly creates anew.

This "turning to the ethics based on the order of nature (stimulated by Brunner) is one of the most excellent things in the Gospel ethics of the present."[9] The understanding of natural orders, however, is at the same time one of the most controversial subjects.

In his *Theologie der Auferstehung* (*Theology of the Resurrection*),[10] Walter Künneth criticizes Althaus' and Gogarten's teaching on the order of creation, a doctrine based on the fundamental separation of Law and Gospel. At the present time in the world, the original state of the order of nature no longer exists as it did in Paradise. Occasioned by man's sin and the grace of God, there remains only the order of God's conservation. In view of this, Künneth prefers to speak only of the order of conservation. The order of conservation is to be understood not from creation alone, for it also has a forward movement in the direction of its final consummation (P. 144). It takes on a symbolic character: a change in a natural event is a symbol of the Resurrection experience (153). Walter Künneth believes that the movement in the political order towards the law of nature is open to a genuinely theological reply from revelation (103). But he shies strictly away from a rational, ontological understanding of the law of nature as applicable to theological ethics. And this, because "the whole structure of a natural-law understanding of being can not be brought into harmony with a view of reality conditioned by revelation" (106). Nature, as it is accessible to us, is no longer "a place where the *lex Dei* (the law of God) in its integrity comes into immediate contact with us" (104). This law itself is defaced and tarnished in its essence and in the way it appears. Therefore, no right has been given to man, "in accordance with his reason and experience," to assert that the order in the world is of divine institution (108).

In his extensive *Ethik des Politischen* (*Political Ethics*),[11] Künneth again takes thoughts from his theology of the resurrection and tries to establish theologically the order of conservation in its trinitarian dimension. The order of conservation has relation to the creation, to the redemption, and to the consummation. Despite the Fall and sin, God, as the Creator and the Father of Jesus Christ, preserves His creation in being. The "order of conservation is the present form of the creative activity of God in the fallen world" (139). Despite sin and corruption, God's salvation-intent is manifested in conservation. Hence, the various orders maintain a definite relationship to the redemption and are "a defense against the diabolical tendency to destruction." In this sense, the order of conservation is also an expression of the angered and chastising God. Yet this chastising role is only the external cloak. Beneath it lies hidden the true reason for God's willing to keep the world in existence, namely, its redemption (139). "Under the Christological aspect, God's anger and punishment, also, become means for seeing to it that the world not remain a sacrifice to sin, but be spared for the action by which God rescues it in salvation-history" (140). Because of sin, as orders of nature they bear also within themselves, ultimately, reference to perfection. They are "interim orders." The created world is "kept in existence with its consummation in view, a consummation having its foundation and promise in the Resurrection of Christ" (140).

With this explanation of the order of conservation, Künneth turns towards that (read Catholic) supra-lapsarian misunderstanding of order. This opinion makes the orders into a second source of revelation. Such a doctrine is false because "in this order there is no question of the original creative will, but of an institution which became necessary because of the Fall" (141). "Man's general knowledge about a fundamental duty and the sanctity of orders and laws in the world" has, to be sure, "formally a similarity with and correspondence to that which God's laws affirm." However, this knowledge of the necessary binding force of this world's laws is veiled, corrupted, and defaced in reference to the divine character of God's Law. But, on the other hand, Künneth also inveighs against the (Melanchthonian) detaching of nature's orders from that area where the divine command holds good. This would result in the orders becoming depersonalized and, thereby, losing all ethical value.

The orders are judged clearly more negatively by Helmut Thielicke.[12] The orders of this universe are neither good in accordance with creation nor neutral in value, "in the sense that they belong to the domain of a law setup that stands squarely at a point beyond good and evil. The truth is, rather, that the orders are the structural forms of a fallen existence" (I,2161). With regard to that order of being which is the foundation of the law of nature, Thielicke argues that, as a consequence of the Protestant conception of sin, not only the knowability, but even its present existence is disputable (I,2122). For, after the fall of man, the order of being "is in such a state of utter confusion that, even in abstract theory, it cannot of itself show forth any intact *ordo*" (I,2184). That is historically verified. Even the history of the law of nature must allow doubts as to "whether anything like the constancy of ultimate norms exists" (I,2087). The image of man and the knowledge of his essence ("abstracting from the God-man relation") appears as inconstant and unpredictable. This relationship, however, between God and man becomes known only in the revelation of Jesus Christ. "Consequently, there can never be had a law of nature that is constant and binding for 'all men' " (I,2092). The problem of fixing limits to things (*Grenzsituation*) shows very clearly that "this universe" is not shot through with "orderly arrangements of creation from which man could establish normative measures." Such objective "states as remnants" of creation do not exist. Those orderly arrangements are simply nothing else than a large-scale mirroring of the human heart. "And just as in this human heart and man's individuality there is little if any dividing line at all that can be fixed between creation and sin, so the possibility is just as slight for doing this on a large-scale dimension of the world" (II/1,695). So the limit-situation (*Grenzsituation*) gives us a pattern for "this world in the most extremely condensed form" (II/1,813). And, on that account, the world can only "be investigated under the two-fold aspect of judgment and grace, law and gospel," in other words, evangelico-theological ethics does not have "to teach the so-called solution of the limit-situation" (II/1,796), but has to strive towards understanding it "rightly."

We are convinced that the thinking of Karl Barth merits greater attention. As we have already said above, Barth utterly rejects the idea of a general revelation. Likewise as a consequence, every point-of-connection between grace and the natural man is thrown out. According to Barth, such admission would radically contradict the unique efficacy of Christ's redeeming grace. In strong Christological concentration, Barth defines creation *formally* as the presupposition (hypothesis) of the redemption, and nature as the presupposition (hypothesis) of grace. In the eternal plan of God for the Incarnation of his Son, creation is included and presupposed. Jesus Christ has eternal precedence prior to and in every act involved in the establishment of the world. A world incorruptible and good in its nature is thereby eternally guaranteed. Because of this, man's existence is, through divine intervention, sheltered from the threat of nonexistence (despair); and that, from the very beginning on, because Jesus truly is the first decree of God.

The hypothesis presents a problem in that, for an understanding of it, the hypothesis must really be considered in the light of the thesis (*Setzung,* existing reality). But, on the other hand, care must be taken against identifying in any way the hypothesis with this thesis ("the presupposition with the existing reality").

The whole doctrine of creation is involved in a twofold impossibility. On the one hand, the order of nature cannot be deduced from the order of redemption. On the other hand, it is just as impossible to separate the orders and to determine from nature below its own essence and meaning. The concept of the hypothesis, therefore, includes a duality of orders. It affirms nothing else than a genuine, but yet only relative, autonomy of the order of nature within the order of grace. Revelation is not creation or a continuation of creation, but an incomprehensible new work of God above and outside of creation (KD I1, 431). Or: "When grace reveals itself, then nature indeed does not cease to be. How could it cease to be, since God does not cease to exist as the Creator of nature? There, within the heart of nature, more than mere nature is to be found;

there nature itself is turned into the display case of grace" (KD II 1,572).

If we question Barth regarding the *material* definition of nature, then he is unable and reluctant to describe for us "nature in itself." This is because he is adamantly against the deduction of such a picture from the order of the redemption. Man, after all, can be explained only by means of transcendence. He is not a being hopelessly enclosed within himself who, by some means completely different from grace, is encountered and by some sort of mental gymnasts made to burst into view.

Man is truly man only insofar as the God-man is his brother. His state is already, therefore, one of union with God. Barth, then, strictly under this condition, expresses what he holds concerning the inner constitution of man's nature. From the vertical point of view, man is a being in contact with God; and, seen horizontally, is a being in contact with his fellow men. The analogy of faith alone (*analogia fidei* as opposed to the *analogia entis*) led Barth to the knowledge of what he sets forth. Thereby is signified an analogous correspondence or proportion between Creator and creature, something which we know only from revelation, therefore, only in faith. From a theological point of view, there is no other approach than this. Thus, Barth can and will describe the visible world only by way of analogy and illustration. Every created thing is but a symbol of the promise and expectation of grace. Every true human being is only one more appearance of Christ. From this dogmatic standpoint Barth now turns sharply against an order of creation which is clear to the natural understanding of every man, and "which would then form something like the basis, the sphere of activity, or the frame for that real human conduct to be inferred from the special revelation of God and made definite by all this" (*KD* III 4, 39).

Yet, on his side, he is prepared

> to admit the concept 'order of nature.' The meaning beneath this would be: The order, namely, the special sphere of divine command and human performance, in which God, who in Jesus Christ is gracious to man, would also rule as the Creator, and there, on the other side, man to whom God in Jesus Christ is gracious, also stands before him as his creature and, through his commandment, would be sanctified and freed. In order to become aware of this order, we need not go beyond the closed circle of theological knowledge (KD III 4,49).

Barth will admit no knowledge of a natural likeness of created being with the being of God; however, he knows about this likeness from revelation. His understanding of the order is "not as an order discoverable by us, but as such an order that is open to us in his Word, and which, when sought after on its side, has as such closed itself off from us" (KD III 4,49). Here it becomes perfectly clear that for

Barth, there can exist no other form of theological ethics than an *ethics of faith* alone. Between nature and grace there can be, according to Barth, no connecting "and." He holds that a theology of law founded upon natural morality is, for that reason, a genuine un-Protestant conception.

When, at the conclusion of the presentation of the Protestant inquiry, we compare the first and last-named (Brunner and Barth) with one another, it might, at first blush, seem that a dialogue, from the Catholic point of view, might be more easily had with Brunner. A closer look at the matter, however, shows that this is, indeed, not so. Admittedly, the conception of a general revelation is one familiar to us. But, on the one hand, the ever-possible opposition between special and general revelation and, on the other, his harking back to the strong antithesis of Law and Gospel make dialogue with Brunner extremely difficult for us. Barth, on the contrary, begins with the Christological salvation-history approach and with the conception of the creature as a presupposition of grace, an idea well-known in St. Augustine.

The historical thought of the great Bishop of Hippo begins with the immediate data of the concrete evidence of the redemption as the fullness of reality and from there goes on to the view of general concepts and their correspondingly narrower degree of reality. Augustine judges from the last act and thereby evaluates natural theology as the revelation of the *Civitas Dei* ("The City of God"). Everything that exists is in its totality subject to the divine providence of salvation. It is directed to the historical salvation-state of Christ and, thereby, stands very completely under the claim of the Church. Thus, salvation-history truly offers a common meeting ground, from which dialogue with Barth concerning the theology of natural law should be possible. The newer Catholic theology also has, on that account, come into the picture here. In the following section this will become still clearer.

THE CATHOLIC VIEW

A. *The Presuppositions of the Present Discussion*

As is true of all present-day theology, so also the Catholic controversy over the law of nature stands under the influence of salvation-history thought. This salvation-history view has its foundation in a harking back to the theology of Holy Scripture (1), and of the Church Fathers (2).

1. The relation of the New Testament ethos to the moral law of nature still needs a great deal more clarification. Hence, this question is directly of the greatest importance for moral theology. If today the whole of theology is increasingly orientated in the direction of Scripture, so a special effort must be made, where the different demands of morality must be grounded, so to speak, "parabiblically."

Let one understand us correctly: we have in mind here not the solution of concrete ethical problems, which are not at all debated in, and, therefore, cannot be immediately answered out of, Sacred Scripture. There is rather a question regarding the fundamental question of the validity of what is generally recognized as human in reference to the biblical image of man. The task of moral theology, in line with the Johannine and Pauline ethics is, certainly, to decide just how the new being in Christ should affect human conduct. Theological anthropology lays the foundation for what moral theology has to say about obligation, the possibility, and norm of moral actions. Granted this, however—of the greatest importance is how far qualities inseparable from the fundamental make-up of man as (evident?) are contained as presuppositions in the biblical image of man and how far they constitute at least a negative norm of morality. In this connection, two points of view seem to us worthy of consideration:

(a) Holy Scripture recognizes the category of "*reestablishment.*" As a foundation for his exhortation to the Colossians and to the Ephesians Paul refers to the man who is renewed in Christ. Thus, it is significant that the renewal takes place "according to the image of his creator" (Col 3:10). The allusion to Genesis 1:25f., together with the parallel passage in the *Letter to the Ephesians* (4:24), clearly refers back to the image on the level of creation. The meaning of the entire passage is certainly this: Christians should mortify that which belongs to the earth, they should not deceive one another, but in patience and love bear with and forgive one another. And all this, because they have arisen with Christ and because, on the occasion of this resurrection and new creation in Christ, *the original man* (without the racial and social differences; compare Col 3:11) *was reestablished*. The result of all this is, then, that there has now also come into existence a man bearing the form of Christ, who should now be intellectually equipped for understanding the logical consequences of this new creation for his moral conduct with regard to his fellow man. The position of Jesus with regard to the question of divorce (Mt 19:3–12; Mk 10:2–12) offers a concrete example for the "reestablishment" of the original order. To be sure, the kingdom of God "in power and glory" is still a future good; but, with the messianic works of Jesus, the great day of final salvation has dawned. Thereupon he proclaimed a new and clear understanding of the will of God. In this connection, he referred marriage also back to the original order of creation. Contrary to the Mosaic permission to issue a bill of divorce (Deut 24:1), he brought into the field those Scriptural passages dealing with the account of creation and concluded from them that, at the beginning of creation, the original will of God held to the indissolubility of marriage. On that account, in the new order, the fundamental statement again indisputably holds good: What God has united into one pair, man should not venture to separate.

> Our Lord refers therewith publicly to the will of God as it finds expression in the visible world about us—namely, to the will of God which is expressed in the nature of man and woman. The law of the indissolubility of marriage is rooted not only in a general way in God's will, but more specifically in the will of God as revealed in the essence of human nature as created by God.[13]

In the New Testament, under a new spirit, this ordered arrangement is again presupposed and its observation demanded. The conception of "reestablishment" through the redemptive work of Christ has its foundation in the fact that, through Him and in Him, "everything has been created" (Col 1:16). Anything that is contrary to the order of creation and, we may add, anything going against man's true nature, cannot fit in with the meaning of redemption. Thereby an answer is not yet given as to whether and to what extent the characteristics of this order, in the sense of actual states of being, are derived from real contact with things outside the mind. In any case, Catholic theology, together with the New Testament, through the activity of God in Jesus Christ, sees at the same time the underlying order of creation as an expression of the one and original will of God sanctioned and strengthened anew.

(b) With regard to the recognition of the will of God from the visible world, today Catholic exegesis coincides largely with the presentation which Emil Brunner makes into a *locus classicus* (Rom 1 and 2). To be sure, Brunner continues to question whether, without further ado, from the *de facto* behavior of man, a true necessity can be made out of that which we believe discovered within man. According to Romans 1 and 2, it seems that the following can be safely held:

1) The invisible essence of God is openly encountered by the Gentiles the same as usual through God's creation, in such a way that the creation *can* be perceived by them intellectually (Rom 1:20). To be sure, *de facto,* the Gentiles do not recognize God from creation any more than they recognize the true God and Creator (Paul stamps them, on account of this, as persons such "as do not know God" [Gal 4:8; 1 Thess 4:5]). In spirit of this—one could speak thus—they still know about God, when they search for a God among the gods. And it is right here that they know also about their relationship to God. Even in their failure to recognize God there is contained another instance of knowledge about God.

2) The Gentiles also know about their responsibility before God. Conscience makes known this claim. It accuses or vindicates man. In this way, according to circumstances, man also knows much about the content of the divine command and about the work demanded by God. And it happens also that he does fulfill the command. To be sure, left to himself as a Gentile, he does not even know this command expressly as a command of the living God; and, on that account, he is inclined in the direction of fulfilling

it as his own proper command in his own proper interest. However, whenever the Gentile or the Jew fulfills in the right sense this command (the will of God), known in this way or otherwise, then the one as well as the other will receive "glory, honor, and peace" (Rom 2:10). In harmony with the entire Pauline teaching on justification, there can never be thereby meant a performance of good actions in virtue of one's own knowledge and power. Without the power of Christ, for St. Paul, all justification is excluded. If, therefore, in the case of Gentiles and Jews, he speaks also of the performance of good actions, this can only take place (this is not contained expressly in the text, but it must follow), through the grace of Christ which works also in the case of the Gentiles. Out of the Pauline doctrine of justification (compare Rom 3:19–24), no question at all can be raised as to whether any justification can take place through the fulfillment or knowledge of the Torah or by means of some natural knowledge. The only justification had is on grounds of faith; but, as to where this faith makes appearance (even in the case of Gentiles), that is another question. By his free grace, God can awaken obedience to faith wherever he will: even, perhaps, also through the law written in the heart of the Gentiles.

2. The thought of the Church Fathers is also full of significance for the present-day discussion. In the first place, we find currently in them what we were already able to

say with our eyes on Sacred Scripture. They look upon the question of the order of creation *from the salvation-history viewpoint.* The first nature created was raised up into the reality of grace, then destroyed through the fall of Adam, and renewed again in Christ. The Fathers repeat this thought many times over. In Christ the original nature has become again visible in its perfection and righteousness. Christ has made known and fulfilled the will of God. As the law of God, His law is also the law of created nature.

> The result is a quite new approach to thinking on the law of nature: the order of nature created according to the will of God, but upset by sin, is reestablished in Christ. Hence, taken materially, the law of Moses and, especially, the Lord's precept of love are identical with the law of nature, which existed in the beginning and which, in the Kingdom of God, will again be complied with in its perfection. The following of Christ and the living according to his law mean fleeing from the corruption of nature, the cleansing of oneself from sin, and, on the day of the perfect redemption, henceforth to become renewed unto the reestablishment of nature and the righteousness of the new man.[14]

A second observation is in order. The theology of the Fathers takes *man's sinful existence* very seriously. Without the grace of redemption, man is a child subject to the wrath of God (Eph 2:3: Anger as the reply of the Holy One to all sins: "to live in darkness" and "to be delivered to the power of the devil"). The state of the sinner means the exclusion from the only real goal of man. The *fundamental essence of* what is right (just) in concrete *human existence* (that which Protestant theology calls nature) consists therein, that man, in this existence, is wholly directed outward towards God and lives a life that flows entirely from the knowledge and love of God. Sin is contradictory to this right direction and means a *fundamental perversion of human existence.* Turned away from God and wrongly turned towards himself—such is fallen man. In spite of all this, man in the state of sin has remained a man. The conservation of the condition of man, which is natural, yet capable of salvation, already signifies the grace of Christ. This grace is signified insofar as the sin, by its own powers, would have destroyed man in his absolute forfeiture of salvation, had not sin been seized upon by the mercy of God. God acted so because sin took place in the order of Christ and remains captive in this order. And so, this domain, one natural yet ruled by Christ, is the place in which sin takes place and the consequences of which will henceforth be checked. In the sinner human nature, still present and healable, is, therefore, not the "abiding remnant of itself still undamaged by sin," but rather is that beginning of salvation in Christ which is already established in continual newness by the graces and kindness of God against sin and its inner tendency for destroying everything. Hence, we must take this fact seriously: the constitution of God's actual world order is a *de facto* unity of two orders. These orders can be really distinguished (and, in spite of their *de facto* union, are also distinct), but *de facto* are not divided or separable (the order of creation and the order of the redemption*).

B. *The Essence and Meaning of the Natural Moral Law*

With the help of this foundation and at the same time keeping in view the classical moral theology, we have accessible to us an understanding of the Catholic teaching on the natural moral law. St. Thomas Aquinas understands the natural moral law principally according to a kind of natural knowledge (*scientia naturalis*). Man possesses an innate tendency through which, without instruction and outside help, he can recognize whatever fundamental demand is made of him for his own self-realization. The expression "naturally" refers, therefore, not so much to an

* In reference to the Augustinian doctrine of the right of nature, Klaus Demmer has recently presented the facts of the case under the special point of view of the analogous method employed by St. Augustine. The Augustinian *theologia naturalis* must be envisaged as a concrete possibility which is founded in the reality of the *civitas Dei* of the free grace of God and can never be divorced from it. Compare K. Demmer, *Ius Caritatis, Zur christologischen Grundlegung der Augustinischen Naturrechtslehre,* Rome, 1961.

objective order of nature and being existing independently of us, but indicates rather the origin of our elementary, rational knowledge. The natural moral law is not an order which of itself is given along with the nature of things and understanding. Thomas proceeds much more from the thought that all being is subject to the eternal law (*lex aeterna,* divine providence) and, on that account, bears within itself a natural inclination for a corresponding norm of life. To a particular degree, this holds good of the essence of the understanding. It also has a natural inclination for a standard of life which corresponds to the eternal law; not, however, in the passive manner of an impressed seal, but in the active sense of the particular concern for oneself and for others (*Summa Theologica* I-II, q.91, a.2: *Sibi ipsi et aliis providens*). God does not drive man nor lead him through instinct, but leaves a share of personal responsibility to every one possessing rational judgment.

The natural moral law is, therefore, in the first and proper meaning, an unformulated law (*lex indita non scripta,* in accord with the New Testament law of grace, *Summa Theologica* I-II, q.106, a.1). It is founded in the obligation and right given to the rational, spiritual person to perform actions which correspond to his being which is in the image of God. As the law of freedom, it is an original gift in man, not through inborn, moral ideas, but formally through the inclination of reason (together with the corresponding tendencies). According to Thomas, man (and actually every individual thing), in his concrete being on the ground of his creaturely quality and in inner analogous unity with the law of grace, has been called to self-realization. Understood in the correct sense, he is truly a law unto himself. In this connection, *ratio* (understanding) means, for St. Thomas, not a simple, natural understanding, in contrast to the light of faith in grace. By reason St. Thomas means much rather a power of grasping reality that is prior to every division of nature and grace.

In this conception, Thomas stands much closer to Paul and Augustine than to Aristotle. The *recta ratio* (right reason) includes the fundamental power of regulating conduct. Thereby Thomas allows this effective knowledge only to those who are Gentile Christians; therefore, he restricts it to the domain of grace.* This effective knowledge has

* For example, this is very clear in the commentary on *The Letter to the Romans* (on Rom 2:14), written shortly after 1259. Compare in this connection, also, K. Demmer, *Ius Caritatis,* 64ff. And his final conclusion: "For Protestant thinking the assertion may be considered hazardous, namely, that Protestant thinkers believe that, in discussion, they are confronted with the problem of a Catholic Thomistic solution of natural theology. This solution, because conditioned by Augustinianism, does not allow the original richness of the Thomistic approach to shine through any longer. The excerpt raises the apparent claim to present the whole reality, namely, that the Augustinian branch-line appears as the main-line of Thomistic thought. Not paying attention to the Augustinian origin allows Protestant thinkers to understand the branch-line, which in Augustinian and Thomistic thinking is thought of only as a *possibility* for salvation, to appear as a concrete *reality* of salvation. This must demand an unconditional return to St. Augustine, in the interpretation of whom the main-line becomes thoroughly vindicated."

an inner relationship to faith as perceptible active union with God. Man's moral knowledge arising, without revelation, from his concrete nature (the law written in the heart, according to Romans 2), is already modified supernaturally. Man realizes that, in virtue of an inner thrust of power, this moral knowledge surges out in the direction of God, the God of the supernatural life. It serves for the preservation of the dignity and the concrete essence of man (together with his relationships in the world). Wherever this "essence and dignity of man is preserved and is realized by individuals in the way enjoined upon them individually at a particular time, there redemption is given through the grace of Christ."[15] Without prejudice to freedom, the achievement of such an act is from the unmerited grace of God. Thus, Christ is truly the point of departure and, at the same time, the goal of all so-called "natural" moral knowledge and of all natural activity. Such thinking does not put any limits on the grace of Christ. Whenever philosophers of religion and phenomenologists discover, as result of rational research, personal conduct, and decisions springing from love, from piety, from primitive trust, from faith, and from hope, they are thus already engaged objectively and subjectively within the sphere of concrete human nature in the grace state. Thereby, they point to an intuition (*auf ein Apriori*), or better to a fundamental existential of the concrete spirit, "that Karl Barth all too offhandedly labeled as 'faith.' This cannot, at any rate, be lumped simply with explicit faith in the authoritative word of revelation, but at the most possesses in revelation its fullness and its own proper individuality" (Balthasar). However, by God's universal salvific will it can be directed towards its proper goal.

With regard to the question of the material content of the norms of the law of nature, it will only be said here that one should not envisage the Catholic law of nature as a collection (*Summa*) of ready-to-hand, unchangeable directives for conduct, deducible from an unchangeable order of nature. Ontological foundation for moral knowledge is, in the proper sense, not an abstract impersonal being, but the concrete, historical man, this person who allows for no substitute. To this extent the contents of moral obligation are nothing else than a "continually necessary and new explanation of the meaning of existence" (Welzel). Only with this data in the background can there be raised the philosophical question concerning the objective structure of being which is prior to and renders human freedom possible. Not everything *de facto* existing in man is by that fact something that absolutely must exist in man. And this is so, also, even though this actually existing reality has a more or less empirical appearance as something universal and changeable only with difficulty. The nature of man, as real, permanent, and necessarily meant to exist can, thereby, be apprehended as such only in a transcendental knowledge and thus be distinguished from the simple, universal reality which happens *de facto* to exist in man. A right of nature deduced from this abstract, metaphysical nature, is, from the theological point of view, a "construction-aid" (*Hilfskonstruktion*), which has its correct meaning in that it can indicate the immutability and universality of certain moral claims. It remains primarily negative and restrictive.

Catholic theology believes that in the reality of creation the continuing creative act can be found and the perdurably creative will apprehended. Catholic theology has confidence that, by coming into contact with the original and abiding will of God contained in Sacred Scripture, it can recognize real intentionality even in perverted creation. It is precisely in the light of this, which is the salvation of the world, that man can, before the salvific will of God, understand creation's lack and need of salvation. This can never mean that we ourselves would be able also to fulfill the abiding challenges of this truth. Only the experience of saving grace in Jesus Christ can let us know with security that the gap can be closed and bridged over between what we know ourselves to be and what we know as our rights and obligations.

II. THE RELATION OF NORM AND SITUATION

Besides the question concerning the validity of the order of creation within the context of New Testament ethics, a second problem is connected with the matter of norms of morality. Namely, since God's will is concrete and definite to the utmost degree, it can and must be right to ask whether this concrete will of God and, thereby, the true demand of God respecting the individual man, can be grasped in general assertions. Were this possible, the will of God "preserved" in human concepts and assertions could be applied in casuistic procedure to individual cases. No one has so clearly and sharply formulated this problem, as has Karl Barth.

> The will of God is concerned as a text ready to hand, partially written, partially unwritten. It has been compiled from the words of the Bible in which it is believed that knowledge can be had of divine ordinances and instructions that are universally valid. Into the composition of this text also go definite, likewise universally valid, obligatory assertions of a moral law of nature which is perceptible to each man in accord with his reason. And, finally, this law-text arises from definite norms which historically have permeated the Christian Western tradition and been affirmed as generally valid. The gathering and shuffling together of the different elements of this text can, consequently, be diversified: the Bible, the law of nature, or tradition can prevail. What really matters is that the command of God be understood in this way or that under the guise of a law-text known both to the ethical teacher and to those under his instruction. Under this presupposition, the task of special ethics consists in presenting the defini-

tions of this law—quite according to the analogy of state law—and to make applications to individual "cases" as they present themselves.[1]

If the moral theologian, on the one hand, has exact knowledge of the law of God under the guise of formulated law-texts and if, on the other hand, he knows about the different possibilities of concrete human conduct, accordingly, in cases of a dubious conscience, he can give himself and others exact advice as to "what must be chosen as good or what must be cast aside as evil" (*Ibid.*). Were ethics thus to be understood, that would mean that the moral theologian would, as it were, put himself on the throne of God.

> He would substitute himself as master, king, and judge where only God can be such. He acts thus on occasion by believing that, in a compendium of moral assertions derived from biblical, natural-law, and traditional sources, after a bird's-eye view he can get to the heart of, pass judgment on the law of God, and thereby can master and manipulate it at will. And, again, he does this also by arrogating to himself such competence in his knowledge of human conduct that it seems possible to him (to him relying on his own mastery of that instrument), to ascribe now this, now that quality to human conduct to the end that it be adjudged before God as good or evil.[2]

This reproach is imputable to the moral theologian no less than original sin, because, with regard to the concrete command of God, which is always the offering of his grace, the moralist tries to strip it of history, of freedom, and of the danger of the lived encounter, and to bring it into a safe haven, in order there, with knowledge of good and evil, to be like God. In this way, casuistry is the wounding of the divine mystery in "ethical experience."

Our question here centers around the relationship of law (general disposition) and experience (concrete calling), of norm and situation. They are to be considered, not as a general ethical problem, but as one of Christian ethics, which is based wholly on Christ, the God-man. This is the problem to which we shall here devote our attention.

NORM AND SITUATION IN PROTESTANT ETHICS

The sharp rejection of every system of casuistry, as we have seen in the case of Barth and as is typical for the Protestant ethics of the present, should not make us think that Protestants, rejecting the presentation and proclamation of general norms, relegate man strictly to an ethical experience in a concrete situation. In the chapter *Law and Gospel* we have sufficiently set forth the fact that the law has meaning for the Christian and his moral life and, consequently, must also constantly be preached to the Christian community. It is solely a question of whether and to what extent the formulated law can be expressed as having binding force over the demanding will of God and whether God, in his absolute sovereign freedom, does not stand above all laws and in the ethical experience, calling man aside, can override all general norms. Protestant ethics has no one pet reply to this. The answer given depends essentially upon the theological position of the individual. Here also, just as in the problem of the natural moral law, theological presuppositions clearly exert an influence. Again, the teaching on the total corruption of human nature shows its unavoidable consequences. General human knowledge centering on fundamental duty, on the holiness of ordinances and laws in the world has even formally a similarity and correspondence to what the commands of God affirm. The laws of this world bear a human character and, hence, man's knowledge of their necessity is hazy, deficient, and indefinite. Nevertheless, the teaching of the supplementary relationship of Law and Gospel becomes clear, especially in the case of Lutheran spokesmen. With regard to the question of norm and situation, there is still another presupposition, namely, certain nominalistic-voluntaristic aspects in the Protestant concept of God.

In the *devotio moderna* (from William of Ockham, 1349, to Gabriel Biel, 1495), a strong emphasis on the sovereign divine will lead to a loosening of the inner, essential connection between God and creatures. With the destruction of the analogy of being there would fall by the wayside also the foundation of an intrinsic, inviolable order among creatures, and inversely the way to the knowledge of the divine will from the created order would be excluded. Human activity sinks down into a chaotic matter which, for want of an inner structure proper to man, takes on meaning before God only through a gracious acceptance by His Will.

Under the influence of Kierkegaard's personalism, it is precisely these thoughts that have enjoyed a strong upsurge within modern Protestant ethics. According to Kierkegaard, man as an individual is freed from the bonds of general categories. His nature takes on a definite character through and from its relationship to God. Existence means being that is had from confrontation with God. In this instance, again, genuine moral responsibility is possible. Neither the categorically imperative nor the idealistic identity-metaphysics leave place for a genuine personal responsibility. In opposition to this, Kierkegaard now stresses (and following upon him the entire Protestant ethics of the present time) that man is responsible only vis-à-vis God issuing a personal demand. Indeed, there is so much stress put on the immediacy of this personal responsibility of the individual before his God, that man can no longer be swayed by the real world surrounding him and its laws, and, actually, no longer even by a general divine "law," but only in the immediacy of an individual "precept."

Besides Kierkegaard's influence, the Kantian ethics takes on great significance. In connection with every rejection of autonomous, rational moral theology, Emil Brunner continues to give testimony to the Kantian ethics:

> The Kantian ethics in this connection (namely: with regard to the question of what man should do) has no simple answer. It evades all prior, material conditions regarding what must be done. That is a characteristic of this system of ethics on account of which (among other aspects), it becomes for us especially worthy of veneration. In particular, the discredited legalism of Kantian ethics, at least not here, gives no evidence of its presence. For this formalism would mean: what is good can, taken materially, in no wise be called such in advance. What is good is obedience actually present.[3]

Brunner would have been ready to adopt this thinking in a modified form: the good right now is obedience to the actually present precept of God.

> With regard to the good understood in the Christian sense, the Kantian formula turns out quite true: 'There is nothing at all, in or outside the world, conceivable as something to be held as unqualifiedly good, with the sole exception of a good will.' Nothing is good except obedience to the command of God, and precisely *because it is obedience.* There is no consideration here

> of a foundation for defining the matter of the law. The 'form' of the will, obedience, is everything. But obedience to the will of God is called: Love your neighbor.[4]

Thus Brunner aims at overcoming the contradiction between materiality and formalism.

In the concrete research of theological situation-ethics, the three presuppositions mentioned (corruption of nature, Law-Gospel opposition, the concept of God) are, with different accentuation, clearly traceable. In the face of every reservation brought up against all forms of grouping and systematizing, we can still distinguish *two directions:*

In the Protestant tradition there is most easily found the type of a relative situation-ethics in which, to be sure, universal norms are recognized. Such norms, however, enjoy only a directive function, a role never to be understood as that of a law. General norms such as these are, in their formulation and communication, necessarily human. Certainly, the sovereign, free will of God is never bound by them. God's personal will is in the highest degree concrete and always reveals itself only in a concrete situation to the believer. The problem (norm and situation) meets us here in the opposition between orders of nature and precept (E. Brunner: *Das Gebot und die Ordnungen*), or between horizontal and vertical (K. Barth). We have already taken up the matter of Brunner: "The 'form' of the will, obedience, is everything." Hence, "the contents of the command is not an abstract law, no previously knowable 'program' to be codified, but permissive self-determination through the Thou in its concrete situation. Love is so 'materially defined,' that no schema can contain what it may well do."[5] The regulations of nature must always be left in suspense before this unpredictable offering of love.

According to Karl Barth,[6] the only course open to ethics is confined to that of a directive to the experience of the concrete command of God and of concrete obedience. And ethics must be on its guard against wanting to give "more than such a directive." The voice of ethics is a recalling to mind of "the authority, the guidance, and the judgment of the Holy Spirit." It is a reminder of "the experience of revelation and of faith which renews itself from one time and situation to the other" (P. 16). "Man's conduct is good, insofar as it is sanctified through God's word, a word that, as such, is also the command of God" (2). However, this command of the living God is "always an individual command for the activity of *this* man at *this* moment, in *this* situation, and is a prescription for *this* man, for his case" (11). Besides this decisive "vertical" of the divine domain there is, of course, also a "horizontal." This means "a steadfastness and continuity of the divine domain that has to be observed as well as of human conduct subject to God's domain" (18).

To be sure, Karl Barth here is clearly different from Emil Brunner. Barth recognizes no fixed, general, perceptible regulations of nature which, in the face of a concrete command, would allow place for an appeal. And he does not admit norms claiming a general (even though not unexceptionable) validity which, however, the concrete will of God could run counter to. With Barth, there is not, strictly considered, any contradiction between norm and situation. He sees in God's command neither a universal command of love, nor a series of numberless, individual revelations each having special form and a special content. So, God's command is indeed here and now actually present to man. However, just as the living, eternal, rich God, is *one,* and not a plurality, "so, he is also therein true to himself in that His command in its infinite, multifold character is not a disconnected plurality of individual commands, but a single command having inner unity" (16). In this way, Barth can now depend upon constancy and continuity in the divine command. The moments, in which this command becomes actual, are indeed moments of divine salvation-history. They correspond to a certain special outlook, which, however, occupies a position securely connected with divine plans in other areas. The meaning of all this is not always revealed to us men. In ethics, we can, indeed, make visible certain constants in the divine domain; but we must always allow them to remain open for the effective will of God, an effective will because it reveals itself only in the concrete situation. From the stability in the divine domain and out of the horizontal, the ethical directive takes on a certain form. And the "task of special ethics is the perfecting, in the way described above, of those norms which are directive with regard to the ethical experience" (18).

Alfred de Quervain understands in a similar manner the relationship of norm and situation. Vis-à-vis God's command, all normative expressions can have only a directive function. This is so, because "God's command is the word, through which God issues commands to us not in a general but in a particular manner."[7]

Also, according to Dietrich Bonhoeffer, God's command "cannot be found or known apart from time or place. It becomes heard only in connection with place and time. God's command is either definite, clear, and concrete to the last degree, or it is not God's command."[8]

What this means in practice should be illustrated through a concrete example. For this we select Karl Barth's position with regard to the medically indicated interruption of pregnancy. We do this because later, with regard to this example, we shall have at our disposition a critical commentary taken from the Lutheran tradition, a commentary which will make especially clear to us the difference between the two types. Barth is very certain that, in every case, "the one destroying fetal life also kills a *man*" (474). In this instance, therefore, first and foremost, the important position of the divine command must be heeded. But this "thou shalt not" is here, in contradistinction to the Roman Catholic "thou shalt not," no abstract law, no absolute prohibition.

> From what premise and from what source should the absolute thesis be founded, namely, that God never and under no circumstances desires anything else than the preservation of a fetal human life? How prove that God can demand nothing else than this from mother, father, doctor, and others associated therein?* God's will is purely his own and he can let this fetal human life die in another way. Could not God, then, in this particular instance also, allow this unborn child to die in this way, inasmuch as these persons and their activity must here and now in this particular circumstance be subject to Him (479f.).

The "thou shalt not" must be heard. The meaning, however, of this "thou shalt not" is the protection of life; and, for the protection of life, there can now be commanded actually the killing of a human being. "Let us speak candidly: there can be situations, in which the killing of the fetal human being is not murder, but is something commanded" (480).

The time and place of such an instance cannot be determined in general, but is revealed only through conscience

* Catholic ethics has never listed the prohibition against killing among absolute prohibitions, which prohibit something that is absolutely bad in itself. God can destroy and give life and can delegate this power also to the State (capital punishment), or to individuals (Abraham). Such a delegation must, in every instance, be examined with the strictest norms by which private revelations are put to the test.

dictated by the concrete situation. Barth bases everything on this point: the safeguarding of God's freedom in his decisions. The negative precept against the taking of human life which comes from the constant norm, "God alone is master of life," does not take away the freedom of God's activity in history. The individual believer must always keep an open mind with regard to whether God actually expects this and not something else from him and, even, possibly exactly the opposite.

The danger of this solution is at once obvious. In his criticism of the Barthian solution, Hendrik van Oyen writes:

> true enough, the statement that the freedom of God is the foundation for our decision seems apparent and clear. Nevertheless, do we but reflect on this matter, the consequences of such a position must also be clear. Namely, how we should act is completely left up to the individual conscience and its perception of the voice of God. And yet, we know how disastrous a hearing like this of the voice of God can be, a voice which can speak so freely, so sovereignly, but, also, so ambiguously.[9]

Today, this systematic search for a solution finds strong support in the biblical theology research into the meaning of the moral instructions in the New Testament. Today it is nearly universally disputed as to whether there is any such thing as a biblical "material ethics."[10] A favorite citation in support of this doubt is the Augustinian *ama et quod vis fac,* "love and do what you will," and this citation is considered as a valid expression of the biblical testimony, that the collection of biblical demands in its entirety should be reduced to and concentrated in the command of love. Thus, all concrete individual commands, as far as their contents go, would be rendered superfluous. "Every system of ethics which affords an answer to the question "what shall I do? and thereby intends to remove from the individual his own reply,"[11] is thereby rendered impossible. The appearance, without more ado, of the list of virtues and vices has to be reckoned as the result of introspective pressure on the part of excessive moralizing.[12] Through the command of love, each individual is appealed to in a concrete situation and when confronted with a concrete individual person. In this confrontation, the one who loves knows how he must realize his love in a constantly new and different way. With that we encounter a "well-nigh enthusiastic understanding of spirit and guidance by the spirit"[13]: "Wherever life and the spirit prevail, a command has no longer any business at all being there" (Lietzmann). The spirit himself points out the way. He is the "adequate ethical guide" (L. Marshall). The one living in the spirit knows from within himself what he has to do and needs no instruction for that. As far as we encounter ethical instructions in the New Testament, we must understand these instructions as concrete examples for the command of love. That holds good for the instructions of Jesus as well as for the Pauline exhortations, of which the "paradigm character" (O. Cullmann) cannot be clearly enough stressed. We cannot here engage in any further discussion of the *Problematik* of biblical ethics. We refer with emphasis to the word of Wolfgang Schrage[14] and admit urgent need for a more adequate Catholic discussion of the Pauline exhortations.

In the Lutheran tradition, while attempting to do justice to the situation-ethics theory, we collided with the *fundamental relation of Law and Gospel* and therewith also encountered the abandonment of an attempt to solve the ethical norm-situation (*Grenzsituation*). The example of the interruption of a pregnancy should again make this clear to us. In this matter, we rely on a very thought-provoking discussion written by Gerhard Stratenwerth.[15] In opposition to Van Oyen (and also indirectly against Barth), he raised the fundamental question. Is this situation possible? "A man actually disobeys a command of God. But, going by other rules, the command of love or whatever, he himself knows no other way out of the situation and disobeys the formal command. And all this, without knowing whether God justifies him on account of his actions." Take the case of the doctor. There remains only the choice either "to think along the lines of Catholic casuistry" and then one may venture nothing (!). Or we must renounce all casuistry and, finally, realize that there is no way possible for giving

> our doctors a good conscience so that they may imagine that what they are doing is allowed. Rather, it is here a case of encouraging our doctors to do what seems to them needs doing and for which they can answer before God. However, being responsible to God for something does not mean approaching His presence as one knowing that nothing else remains for God other than to say: "Go away, you have acted rightly!" Accountability before God for something means laying something at His feet and then awaiting and accepting his judgment.

In this example an actual clarification of the demand in the norm-situation (*Grenzsituation*) is fundamentally out of the question, because then the one on whom a demand is placed can only just presume that he is acting rightly. This solution follows along the lines laid down by Helmuth Thielicke, whose attempt must be here presented in really much broader extent.[16]

Under various cautionary provisos, Thielicke holds the norm for the average case as completely knowable and realizable. Indeed, ethics holds good actually only on the boundary-or-conflict cases (for example, in the conflict between life and truth; between life and life, between general public and oath of fidelity). This conflict he calls fringe-situation (*Grenzsituation*). in the *Grenzsituation* there is a question of the properly ethical decision. In this situation, the ethical adviser must be thoroughly discreet. "When he has a personal decision or other to be carried out, a decision incommunicable to others because it is not based on an objective standard, he may not venture to make this binding also upon others" (II/1,757). Here, also, the moralist is clearly encountering the limits of his field. The *Grenzsituation* is, frankly, signally clumsy. It constructs "a model 'of this world' on the smallest possible scale" (813). On that account, it can undergo a theological investigation only under the double aspect of Law and Gospel, of judgment and grace. Ethics has not, in that connection, to teach the so-called "solution" of the *Grenzsituation* but "to put up with and to understand it" (796). The *Grenzsituation* deprives men "in a brutal manner of every opportunity to become righteous through works" (813). "I have in faith to hold out for forgiveness. At this point, ambivalence of the word of God as Law and Gospel is revealed in the situation and confers on it an ambiguity that, theoretically, is insoluble" (804). Such, therefore, is the presentation that the conflict-situation makes of itself for ethics and this is the way it must be seen "from outside": the ambiguity of the demand and the conflict emerging out of the *simul iustus et peccator* (righteous and sinner at the same time) cannot be taken away.

For those themselves who are in the midst of the conflict, Thielicke puts his confidence in the help of the Holy Spirit: The one consigned to the conflict sees himself cast into the state of worry, as to whether he will grasp the situation objectively and rightly understand the *status confessionis* latent in this situation, and whether he will be in the position for the discernment of spirits. "This complication characteristic of the anticipating, analyzing reflection, will . . . at a definite moment be resolved through the help of the Holy Spirit by a clear simplification, that is by the revelation of an unequivocal alternative" (1092). God himself now enters into the plan and takes over responsibility for this, His affair, "and thereby also for the answer which is given in obedient and trusting openness. Man is not a soloist, but a part of the cast" in the struggle for the kingdom of God against the power of anti-Christ. "The Spirit himself puts in an appearance and engages in the conflict" (1093). Thus, in simple "clarity" we are advanced to the front of the struggling kingdom of God (1103).

We now have to break off our presentation of the Protestant effort to solve the ethical situation. In this compressed (and dangerously so) brief synopsis, it has surely become apparent to us that here great and truly Christian positions have entered into the discussion. Such, namely, as: the living, personal call of God; giving faithful heed to the guidance of the Holy Spirit; the knowledge of one's own insufficiency; the renunciation of every form of moral self-righteousness. How far is Catholic moral theology ready to take over these positions as a legacy for itself? That is our next question.

NORM AND SITUATION IN CATHOLIC MORAL THEOLOGY

Were one to affirm that it was only most recently for the first time that Catholic moral theology took cognizance of the role of the situation in the ethical decision, we would have to reject that as a gross mistake. The teaching on circumstances as a source of morality always tried to take into consideration the factor of the situation in the framework of the law of morality. Furthermore, the classical teaching on the moral law contains astonishing first-beginnings for an ethics of personal responsibility. As a result of this, today, in the dialogue with existential philosophy and with the Protestant ethics, also new beginnings along this line (have been developed).

The first point of departure in Catholic thinking for the putting into order of concrete demands lies in the proper understanding of the moral law. We have already dealt with that extensively in the first chapter.

The first and real law of the Christian, the law of Christ (Gal 6:2; 1 Cor 9:21) is no written law. It signifies much more the duty and claim for corresponding conduct which is received with our being "in Christ" or "in the Spirit." The moral imperative is found in the positive promise of the grace of God. "We are created in Christ Jesus in good works, which God has made ready beforehand that we may walk in them" (Eph 2:10). "The norm for moral theology is the fulfilled εἶναι ἐν Χριστῷ, 'being in Christ,' not a cosmos or even only a collection of norms of action."[17] The positive assertion of the newly acquired existence of Christ is imperative in its urgency for action.

"Existence" means here *concrete salvation-existence,* not a Christian existence in general. Rather, it is the sharing in the history of Jesus Christ, in a history which, according to St. Paul, is shared with *every individual man,* at the moment of his arriving at faith and being baptized. For each individual man, baptism signifies a fundamental changing, a real regeneration, which man experiences ever anew in his faith. He has been taken into a new history and his old history, out of which he came, has come to an end. "We were buried with him by means of baptism into death, in order that, just as Christ has risen from the dead through the glory of the Father, so we also may walk in newness of life" (Rom 6:4). This duty and claim vested in man, as it is revealed in individual moments (*kairos*) of the individual salvation-history of the Christian in the concreteness of its contents, is what is meant by the "law of Christ." It is also called "the law of the Spirit of the life in Christ Jesus" (Rom 8:2).

The Christian does not give heed to a host of commands, which come upon him from without and with which certainly he cannot correspond. Rather he hearkens much more to the voice of the Spirit which, at one and the same time, urges him towards and strengthens him for the performance of good actions. "Thus, the 'law of the spirit' is not a new codex of laws, but rather an urging towards good proceeding from the Holy Spirit."[18] Thereby the meaning of the apostolic exhortation (*Paränese*) should not be taken away, but will be put back into the proper perspective. The "law of the spirit" finds its fulfillment in love. It refers back so clearly to the preaching of the chief commandment through Jesus, just as Paul also in other connections refers to the instructions of Jesus (Compare 1 Cor 7:10, 25; 9:14; 14:37).

Christ did not take away the law but he fulfilled it. And now he calls and strengthens us to fulfill it in him. According to the side of the material content, there exists an inner continuity in reference to the preeminent principle of the will of God and, in the command of love, of the close connection between the "Old" and the "New" Law.[19] This holds good not only for the Master's Sermon on the Mount, but also for the Pauline exhortation. To the extent that, in the New Testament, we encounter general, formulated demands, these same demands must always be understood and fulfilled in reference to the law of the Spirit of the life in Christ (Rom 8:2).

Our excursus on Thomas Aquinas' doctrine on law has shown that this is not simply knowledge resulting from the latest biblico-theological research, but already represented the best teaching of scholasticism.[20] We have to understand the so-called natural law as having inner unity with the law of Christ. Analogous to the law of grace, the natural law is also principally no written law (*lex scripta*), but a law bestowed upon the heart (*lex indita*). As we have seen, the rational spiritual person has a natural being formed in the image of God. With this nature there is given a duty and right for corresponding conduct and it is in this that the natural law is founded. This duty-right quality united with the concrete man must be seen in unity with the Christian salvation-existence. Our existence does not lie under a heap of external precepts; rather, we have to actualize personally that which we ought to be, in accordance with what we are told by God, creation, and redemption.

Hence, the entire man, the redeemed man, in his absolute uniqueness, in the intimate relationship of nature and grace, is the one called to account by God.

A second point of departure lies in the personal ethics of being, as it is expounded today by outstanding scholastics. J. B. Lotz stresses the following: today, the *ontology of being,* under the dominance of material reality, must be confronted by an *ontology of existence* ruled over by the concept of person. In the intellectual life of the West, the ascendency of the ontology of being may well have stemmed from the Greeks. "But today the turning point seems to have been reached when the ontology of existence under the rule of person, is taking over the leadership for the future of Christianity."[21] The moment an ontology devotes itself to being, it runs the risk of understanding being in the light of material things. The consequence of this, then, will be that the person also will be likened to a thing and its inner structure or be understood as a thing of more perfect kind, and, consequently, will be deficient in its proper characteristics. It is much better that an ontology proceed from the concept of person. The relationship of being as such appears on reflection in the concept of person alone. The material thing, also, can be explained in the light of the structure of person. "With the person's growing dim, the material thing becomes bright, if it is shot through with light coming from the person."

Without its thereby being taken out of the order of being, person is now quite otherwise referred back to the point of departure. A system of values will be set up only and precisely through the communication of existence to person. It is in virtue of this system of values that the kingdom of being is an ordered hierarchy of good things.* Thereby an approach is also opened up for looking upon the individual not simply as one out of a class of beings, but rather, also, in his uniqueness, in his personal worth which is not communicable out of the specific group, but which has its foundation in his being called by God. This singular proper being of the individual and his individual worth stands, as

* Consideration should be given as to what this means for the prevailing discussion of the personal structure of marriage. Compare L. M. Weber, *Mysterium Magnum. Zur innerkirchlichen Diskussion um Ehe, Geschlecht und Jüngfräulichkeit* (*Quaestiones disputatae* 19), Freiburg, 1963.

does all being, under the binding will of God. That which is positively individual, insofar as it is more than the "case" of the general, certainly belongs fundamentally to the content of the concrete demand. Accordingly, the concrete obligation is not only a case and application of a general law, also not *merely* an especially typical case, but it is much more like an individual call and, likewise, demands an individual answer.

In accord with these presuppositions, we can now say the following with regard to the question of norm and situation:

1. God, as *Ens concretissimum* (the most concrete Being), makes demands of man, not in general, but in the concrete. His call holds good always in ultimate concreteness for a concrete man and demands an answer in faith and love. In the history of salvation, this answer always means grace, which calls man to and gives him strength for conversion and for sanctification. This call is not, primarily, to be understood as a verbal inspiration. It comes to self-expression, much more primarily, in the salvation-history being of the entire man who has been called to self-realization.

2. This unique and personal call of God discloses itself in this positive uniqueness only to an unobjective, properly personal knowledge. In relation to the law of grace, it is sanctification in faith and in love given by God. Thus, therefore, in its positive uniqueness, the moral obligation

cannot be known as capable of expression through thoroughly "objective," that is, universal concepts. To this extent, there is had no ultimate, general, material determinability of good and evil.

3. Another question is whether we have no legitimate approach at all to the concrete command of God. Catholic ethics holds fast, in this question, to the possibility and validity of certain general norms. It is even, to be sure, the first task of every scientific system of ethics to uncover and hold firmly such norms. Some such general instructions can be derived from the word of revelation in Scripture. Our exegetes, with their modern methods, can help us in whatever way they like towards achieving this in a neat, critical manner. But such norms can, also, be brought to light with the help of the human understanding enlightened by faith. In the second and derived sense, the natural law, in this way, appears also as formulated law. This is true, inasmuch as, under the presupposition of a law of nature which is knowable and binding on all man, general, obligatory, fundamental laws of conduct can be derived from the permanent structure of this nature.*

* Here, anew, there arises the theological *Problematik* of the possibility of such derivations from concrete (fallen) nature. Nature, that is, the abiding structure of man, insofar as it is the foundation and the declared norm of his conduct, belongs to the ensemble of the one, super-

These laws, formulated and in this sense effected from without, whether they be natural-law propositions or ordinations of the New Testament, are, in any case, never the definitive and appropriate instructions for the child of God. They signify, nevertheless, in a negative formulation, the restrictive limit, the death-line under which the will of God can never be found.

Turning to our example of the interruption of pregnancy should clear this up somewhat. The demand that God makes

---

natural reality of creation. If sin destroys man even in his fundamental right-being-before-God (what Protestant theology calls nature) (*τέκνα φύσει ὀργῆς*, Eph 2:3; also, the Second Council of Orange can. 22, D 195), even so, there still remains that core of nature which precisely Catholic theology entitles nature (*natura metaphysica*), on which this theology bases its derivation of general assertions. This nature was assumed by Christ's being truly man and is included in the Christian image of man. It forms in the totality of the redeemed man, as it were, the substratum for that which is the real, for the supernatural. Since moral theology derives its norms systematically from dogmatic anthropology, the natural-law claims are likewise included therein; yes, it is only therein that they maintain their deepest and ultimate meaning. Hence, a right of nature derived from man's metaphysical nature has, indeed, a meaning that corresponds to the actual state of affairs (the task of ethics). But, viewed theologically, there is but question of a construction-aid (*Hilfskonstruktion*). This has its good (true) meaning in this, that it indicates the immutability and universality of certain, moral demands. But, it remains primarily negative and restrictive. As the abstract, metaphysical concept of nature was converted into a formally theological concept, for the purpose of getting a more exact understanding of the biblico-salvation-history concept of nature, in like manner, this understanding must be understood of the biblico-salvation-history claims.

of a doctor in a particular situation is, as far as man can find out, limited by the proposition that a man may never, just because he has full power to do so, dare do away with an innocent human life.* Positive propositions, however, oblige us to refer to a scale of values, which, in the decision, have to be pondered, to be weighed against one another, and then to be realized—in our example, something like this: professional employment of all possible and licit means, uprightness, goods to be obtained, and so forth. The negative death-line or -boundary and the clearly defined possitive references to values that are to be acted upon and made a reality—together, these lay down the limits for an area of action in which the command for the performance of an action in its ultimate concreteness can and must be discovered by that man alone upon whom the imperative is imposed.

It is evident that ethics as a science is much more occupied with the law than with the developed, lived morality. As a science, ethics can express only in a general concept what holds good for the individual good action. On the contrary, the individual good in a completely different way is immediately accessible to the prudence and the judgment of

* Since, with regard to the prohibition against killing, there is not involved an absolute prohibition (compare asterisked note on p. 97), for this reason negative norms must be conditionally formulated here. The example of lying would be to the point. Because God can not lie, he can also never found a lie in his will. "Not to lie" would be an absolute limitation.

the conscience of the individual. Here there is question concerning the absolute obedience to the grace-guidance of the Holy Spirit and the prudent discernment of spirits. That is the position of formal existential ethics which is understood by Karl Rahner as a complementary concept for a general essential ethics.

Existential ethics endeavors to indicate,[22] how the position of existential philosophy, the self-realizing of the person in the events of the situation, and the insistence of Protestant ethics on a constant hearkening to the concrete call of God, how all these can be considered in a legitimate form also within Catholic moral theology. Thus, against all nominalistic-voluntaristic extremes, such a system of ethics would hold firmly to the validity of general norms. However, it also recognizes the limits which are inherent in every general norm on account of its essentially abstract character with regard to the communication of the concrete thing demanded. The moral imperative, taken as the concrete call of God, has for the man subject to such a call always a fullness of contents that goes beyond a rational, deductive definition. So, in this way, existential ethics can lead pure essential ethics out of the danger of "legalizing." And it can point out to the individual Christian how the only way he is able to recognize as the true good the will of God placing him personally under obligation is if he is willing to listen to God's call to the very end, yes, even to remain with his very existence drawn into the drama.

A person can understand only to the extent that personal

faith and surrendering love remain the foundation and highpoint of all considerations. This is true just because faith and love are a sharing in the divine life and the God of grace cannot be recognized without the God of grace. Only a personalism which thus clearly gets its understanding from the God-man can be a check to the constantly underlying danger of a hidden egoism.

CHAPTER 3

SINNERS AND SIN

As our first choice in the fundamental questions of theological ethics we selected the question of law. The course of development of the ethics of evangelical theology is consequent upon the dogma of the redemption by Christ the unique Mediator. With that starting point, Protestant theology is keenly aware of the danger of excessive legalizing. Its fears are: the Christian, helped by the fulfillment of the law, might attempt to effect a claim to his own salvation. On the contrary, we hold fast to a truth that the demands of God have their foundation in his self-communication through grace and, consequently, their fulfillment in obedient love also represents always a fruit of grace.

Evangelical theology gives us further warning against hastily believing that man could adequately enclose the will of God in propositions in order to apply them casuistically to individual cases. Contrariwise, proceeding from the Catholic point of view, we have to hold firmly to the fact that the New Testament, nonetheless, does contain a series of concrete demands, the contents of which also have general validity for Christians. It is, however, as the result of painstaking work on the part of exegetes that these demands are to be established. In conjunction with the so-called natural law, these precepts could enable us, in every instance, to indicate the lines of demarcation between deadly egoism and self-sacrificing love. These precepts also give us a sure point of reference for the discovery of the good in its fullness as determined by the concrete situation.

Starting out from here, we have an open door to the question of sin with which we shall be engaged at the closing of this work. It is easy to see that Evangelical theology, by its rejection of casuistry, emphasizes not so much sins, as it does sin and, consequently, the sinner. Therewith, Protestant theology issues a warning (one to be taken seriously) in the direction of post-Tridentine Catholic moral theology. For this theology, with eyes fixed upon the sacrament of Penance and the function of the confessor, has been overly satisfied with the presentation of sins in their moral differences. As before, in two stages, there will first be a presentation of the Protestant position and then the Catholic attempt at an answer.

Evangelical theology stresses emphatically man's fundamental sinful state lying behind every actual sin. The essence of sin is not properly exhausted by limiting it to man's abnormal actions and desires. The roots of sin are buried much deeper in a corrupted fundamental composition of man, from which the individual abnormal desires and actions continually come forth, so that the real roots of sin lie deep within the essential core of man. The *commission* of sin, therefore, always comes, indeed, from the *being* a sinner. Evangelical theology devotes its greatest attention to this being a sinner.

> Sin, in its root meaning, is not an inner, anthropological category (that is, human perversion measured by a self-sufficient ideal norm of men), but a strictly theological category. That is, sin is the perverted, fundamental condition of man in his relationship to God, in the God-relation. This theological perspective of sin, as properly their own, will be tirelessly insisted upon by the Lutheran confessional writings against a merely moral or an inner-anthropological, fundamental composition of sin.[1]

Thereby—as E. Kinder further explains—neither is every good denied to the natural man (the natural moral possibilities are maintained), nor should it in any way be said that in the bath of regeneration the man-made righteous is not truly made righteous. On the contrary: "the ban of the angry judgment of God which got expression in the original sin of man, is broken with regard to the baptized person. Such a man has approach to the Father and therein—in the union with God—has freedom from original sin."[2]

> The statement about original sin is, therefore, not a derogation of human, creaturely worthwhileness, nor an expression of human inferiority, be it biological, intellectual, or of the moral character type. It is, rather, an expression concerning the relationship to God, in which man stands with the fundamental act of his person and with the fundamental constitution of his existence.[3]

It must, therefore, be said outright that man by *himself* is capable of no type of self-justification; and it must be pointed out of what deep dimension our actual sins break forth and in what depths of existence they threaten man continually anew. The search cannot and must not be here undertaken as to what extent the education of children corresponds to the collective evangelical persuasion. We wish to hear the position which is also rooted in the Catholic tradition.

The Counter-Reformation has continued to maintain the Scotistic argument: *Naturalia manent integra in peccatore* (the natural gifts remain intact in the sinner). It made this position its own, so that the original sin consists only in the deprivation of sanctifying grace, as decorative accidents. According to biblical concepts, man without the grace of redemption is a child of wrath (Eph 2:3); he lives in the state of remoteness from God and abandonment. He is excluded from the one real goal to which he was called. The sin of our first parents has corrupted man in his fundamental right being before God (according to the evangelical understanding; in his nature—that is, in his being an image of God). Admittedly, the essential core of man's nature remains preserved in an undamaged condition. This is what Catholic theology designates as the essential nature (*natura metaphysica*) being in the image of the creature. But the true human existence, as God willed it, is lost. This can only consist in this that man lives entirely out of the knowledge and love of God.

Original sin means the loss of righteousness, in a word, of an existence directed toward God; and, because of this, it means a fundamental perversion of the true human existence directed toward God; and, because of this, it means a fundamental perversion of the true human existence as God willed it. Man, whose entire existence depends upon the love of God, this man in the first sin, turned himself away from that foundation of his existence and, thereby, lost the foundation of his existence. Turned away from God and perversely directed towards himself, that is man existing by himself. Thus he merits that the earth should snatch him away, that he be instantly damned.

According to St. Augustine, the sin of Adam has made the whole of mankind into a "*massa damnationis*" (mass of damnation).[4] And Canon 22 of the Second Council of Orange (D 195) defined that everything that man has from his own proper resources, and not from a merciful grace (in the widest sense) is a sin (*de suo nisi mendacium et peccatum*). And if, in consequence of his sin, man is not destroyed at once, his thanks for that must go out to the presence of Christ, to Christ already abiding as *man,* abiding in whom and unto whom everything has been created (Col 1:16).

In his reply to Karl Barth, Hans Küng performed his greatest service by bringing again to light in a greater Christological view the ancient tradition of the Church concerning the lost state of man. Man has remained man, the destructive power of sin has been taken away, not in any way through the constancy of man, but only in Christ.

> The *terminus a quo* of the event of justification is, therefore, the sinner. That means not a man, who out of his own power has continued in some way or other to hold his own, who even without Jesus Christ could have continued to exist 'as man,' and, thus, would have preserved for himself a final autonomy. Much rather, the sinner is that man who, for all the human existence that, in spite of sin, has remained with him, has to thank Jesus Christ who has preserved it for him unto his justification. Accordingly, the sinner—in spite of his power of choice—is capable on no level at all of any kind of justification whatsoever.[5]

Therefore, from beginning to end, our righteousness is one that is given to us. It is one that comes to us from above and from without. It thereby is also a justification given to us really as our own belonging, but not as belonging to us from within. It is given "as a justification proper to another" (*propria, sed non tanquam ex nobis propria,* D 809). As a consequence, for our moral preaching, the following results from this:

1. We must emphatically point out to man the deep dimension of sin. Jerome Regnier believes[6] that, through our "moralistic extrinsicism," which sees in sin, principally, a willful offense against the law, we bear a large share of the blame for modern man's having lost his sense of sin. This moralistic extrinsicism is not, however, thereby overcome in that we identify the objectively theological concept of sin, the *aversio totalis completa a Deo* (the total turning away from God), with a particular selected instance of a violation of the objective order. On the contrary, we must first of all make a much sharper distinction between the theological essential concept of sin and the moral theological expression for the gravity of a violation of the objective order. "A sin is a mortal sin when a choice is made *against love*. Wherever such a radical contradiction to the love of God or neighbor is not present, sin cannot be a mortal sin."[7] *Sin, in the proper sense, is always and only there had, where the love, the relationship of men to God is destroyed.* With this relationship destroyed, the foundation of our true, human existence is also destroyed. In this sense, the fundamental essence

of sin, as a radical "no" against God's will is always the same.

Without doubt, then, sin is specified in individual acts, each according to the material that is taken out of the multiple world of values, in which this "no" is realized. Moral theology classifies and evaluates this "material" and, at the same time, passes a practical judgment: a particular ("this or that") inordinate conversion to a creature contradicts the will of God, and, thereby, may be apt for provoking on the part of man an essentially radical decision against God. In general, we can by no means say definitively whether this results actually in a total decision; but, in our customary practice, we act as though we could. Egotism contains existential degrees, which are expressed in the inordinate conversion towards a creature. Only the person who devotes himself completely to a created good, who chooses it as the center of his life (*tanquam finen et centrum universale!*), destroys completely his ordination towards God. If we but fix the limits more clearly of this last dimension of sin, we will devote much more attention and importance to the tepid, indifferent, ungrateful and egotistic conduct in our "friendship with God," as it finds expression in the so-called venial sins.

2. As our concept of sin increases in depth, we must become increasingly aware of the fact that, as sinners, we continually stand in need of redemption by God. Among men of today sin is the object of much discussion. In novels

and on the stage man subjects himself to a much sharper criticism than any ponderous preacher of penance would dare to indulge in.

Our modern literature and psychology are shot through with a frightening effort to plumb the evil that dwells in the conscious and unconscious depths of the human soul, even to peering into its most secret abysses and hiding places. But "present-day man, who allows himself to be held up by poets and psychologists before the mirror of his wretchedness, is not at all pleased that he be accused of sin by anyone, not even by the Church in the name of God Himself."[8] The expressions of modern moralization are not concerned with knowledge of the state of sinful man nor with the activity of the Holy Spirit when he convicts the world of sin (Jn 16:8). Hence, he is able neither to bear the blame, nor to overcome it. With a shrug, he tries to put the blame on fate and destiny; or, finally, he explains it by absurdity, which Camus says all know to be nothing other than "the consciousness of the sinful without faith in God."[9]

The opposite of this also holds good, namely, the continually pointing out in Christian preaching of the need for redemption. There is an underlying difficulty here: namely, because of infant baptism, we scarcely any longer bear within us the tremendous experience of conversion. We are greatly lacking in a lively awareness of what an abyss and what a state of being lost we have been saved from by God's free grace of redemption. We must continually be conscious of the truth that no one simply "has" grace, but that grace only then can be truly "maintained" by one's being ready and willing for a continuous reception of it in the future. Grace is not simply placed at our disposition; it is continuously being given to us; I, and I who of myself am nothing else than a sinner (D 195), continually receive the favor and love of the Holy Spirit. Or, as St. Thomas has put the matter: "*Deus semper operatur justificationem hominis sicut sol semper operatur illuminationem aeris* (God is continually in process of justifying man, just as the sun is always bringing out light for the air)."[10]

3. As a consequence of the strong emphasis placed upon the sinful state of man, evangelical theology demands a continuous conversion: the *transitus* ("the passing over") from sinner to righteous man. Two aspects can be clearly seen in Luther's expression, *simul iustus ac peccator* (at the same time a righteous and sinful man). At one time, he calls man *totus iustus—totus peccator* (completely a sinner—completely a righteous man). At another time, however, he calls him also *partim iustus—partim peccator* (partially a righteous man—partially a sinner). Countless expressions point in the direction of the total aspect. The *simul* means, in this connection, "not the equally important position of the component parts of a two-piece moment of time, with the parts thereof mutually restricting one another. It is rather the place where the two-part whole struggles for self-exclusion."[11] Yet, the self-exclusive predicates belong to

a completely different level of being: man is entirely a sinner *sub specie sui ipsius* (in reference to himself), and completely righteous *sub specie Christi.* In this connection, however, it must never be forgotten that Luther is not describing a state of being; on the contrary, his desire centers totally on proclaiming *the way* traveled by the Christian from sin to his sanctification, "in the act of his hearing God speak to him."[12] This *transitus* from me to Christ, from my existence as a sinner to God's salvation-existence for me, is never a reality, ready-to-hand and already consummated, but a movement which is to be perfected right now continually anew. It is a movement which, as long as life remains in the flesh, will never come to an end.

At this point Luther speaks also of the partial-aspect of the *simul. Lex docenda est tam piis quam impiis, quia pii partim iusti sumt, partim peccatores*[13] ("the law must be taught to pious people as well as to those who are not, because pious people are partly righteous, partly sinners"). The *simul* means sinners in their state of being that is prone to sin, but no longer such in will and in act; *iustus* means one indeed righteous in will and inchoatively already in act, but not yet righteous in the sense of a spontaneous state of being good surging forth from within.

A *progressus*-aspect of the Christian life accompanies the *transitus*-aspect. This is somewhat as in the picture of the "*aegrotus samaritanus,*" tirelessly cited by Luther, and of the sick man who, under the care of the Samaritan, gradually regains his health. There is and remains on earth only a beginning and an increasing,"[14] a *moveri de bono in melius velut aegrotus de aegritudine in sanitatem* ("moving from good to better as a sick man from sickness unto health").[15]

Here, once more, we are not concerned with a judgment, or, still less, a justification of the Lutheran pronouncement. The *transitus* of the sinner in the doctrine of imputation may, possibly, have been heretically distorted and emptied of content. Our wish, at this point, is only to give a full hearing to the legitimate position which the evangelical teaching conceals within itself. Even though made righteous, we are still but sinners. Through our having been forgiven, we have been freed from the *reatus culpae,* that is, the guilt involved in sin was blotted out. Sin, however, was not thereby as an *historical experience* made null and void. For what once happened remains forever an element in the history of man.

Accordingly, our position is one of continual struggle. Within ourselves, we are reduced to tension in a genuine history of the daily turning away anew from the old and tending out towards the new man. We have actually been redeemed and made new in the Lord (2 Cor 5:17), but we do not yet possess "the perfect manhood, to the mature measure of the fullness of Christ" (Eph 4:13). Our stand is in the constant tension between beginning and final redemption. Actual sins, as possibility and fact, are still permitted to us. For the one made righteous, the power of sin is, to be sure, fundamentally broken; but the lust of the heart has remained. In Chapter Seven of the *Letter to the Romans,* the portrayal of the man who is riven in soul and struggling holds good actually today (according to the majority of interpreters), of the unbaptized and unconverted man. But many exegetes insist, Paul wrote his statement of the impossibility of following reason, not without a side-glance at the believer and the baptized person.[16] Assuredly, our existence in faith is in movement like that of the one in the race (1 Cor 9:24). And, indeed, it is qualified as the movement from the past and the turning towards that which is to come. This has not to do with a mere holy "preservation of the state of grace," but with the daily decay for the outer and renewal for the inner man according to 2 Cor 4:16 and of an ever new conversion (Hebr 3:7).

In the concrete, what is the meaning of this for our preaching of morality? In our presentation of what we ask of people, do we take sufficiently seriously the fact that our Christian life is that of the wayfarer? No doubt can be had about *the goal of conversion:* it has to do with the evermore perfect presentation of who the Christian is and must evermore so become because of his being inserted into Christ as a member. Speaking out, however, about *the way and time* of conversion is much more difficult. Deeply impressed by his past sins and the resultant, abiding tendency towards sin, man needs time for the maturing of self and the understanding of the claims of God. Through baptism and grace, our nature is certainly not wholly changed. It must first slowly be weaned away from itself, in order to undertake and perform whatever is laid before it as having an objective and legitimate claim upon the soul. Because, even through the sacrament of Penance, a sinful past is not simply blotted out, it is indeed quite possible for a man suddenly to consider an objectively valid claim as not binding him because, with more or less blame on his side, he refuses to have anything to do with it.

We must understand and take seriously this sinful state of being. Just as sure as the guilt can be wiped away only by God, it is likewise certain that conversion, while being a work of grace, is still, however, a completely human, historical process. Every step forward in it has its opportune moment for grace. In our moral preaching, it is our obligation to proclaim, without restriction, the claims of God, and to present a great ideal as an objective norm for action. We are, however, neither judges in a criminal court, nor promulgators of a heavenly book of penal law, which, by its laws, demands of man the carrying out of concrete actions and, correspondingly, metes out to them reward or punishment.

Man, considered in himself, is always the one in charge of things. To be sure, *Deus impossiblia non iubet* ("God does not command impossible things"); of this Catholics are convinced. God gives men sufficient grace (*gratia sufficiens*); otherwise, becoming truly guilty would become out and out impossible. But, in the Council of Trent, the meaning goes farther: *Iubendo monet et facere, quod posses, et petere quod non possis et adiuvat ut possis,* D 804, ("in issuing orders, God admonishes us both to do what we can and to ask for that which we cannot do; and God helps us that we may be able to do it"). There is such a thing as a human *non posse* (human incapability); and only through long and persistent prayer can this be turned into a grace-filled *posse* (an ability). Hence, under the demand of God, for the very first time, man becomes conscious of his being in a sinful state and of his deep need for redemption. And he experiences, to a degree, something of the genuine meaning of the *simul peccator et iustus!*

FOOTNOTES

Chapter 1: LAW AND GOSPEL

[1] WA 36.9.

[2] W. Joest, *Gesetz und Freiheit, Das Problem des Tertius usus legis bei Luther und die neutestamentliche Paränese,* Göttingen, ^{2}1965, 9.

[3] W. Joest, *ibid.,* 9.

[4] E. Wolf, *Gesetz und Evangelium, dogmengeschichtlich: RGG^{3} II, 1523.*

[5] E. Wolf, *ibid.*

[6] H. Schlier, *Der Brief an die Galater,* Göttingen, ^{11}1951, 106.

[7] H. Schlier, *ibid.,* 108.

[8] Compare W. Joest, *op. cit.,* 21–36, and the critical questions apropos thereof in H. Gollwitzer, *Zur Einheit von Gesetz und Evangelium,* Antwort (Festschrift for Karl Barth), Zurich, 1956, 297 f.

[9] K. Barth, *Evangelium und Gesetz: Theologische Existenz heute, Neue Folge,* 50 München, 1956 (original edition, 1935).

[10] E. Wolf, RGG^{3} II, 1525.

[11] Compare E. Brunner, *Der Rechtfertigungsglaube und das Problem der Ethik: Gott und Mensch, Tübingen,* 1930, 24 ff.; H. Thielicke, *Theologische Ethik,* Tübingen, 1958, I, 28–33.

[12] F. Lau, "Gesetz, ethisch," RGG^{3} II, 1527.

[13] W. Joest, "Gesetz und Evangelium," RGG^{3} II, 1527.

[14] W. Joest, *ibid.*

[15] K. Barth, *op. cit.,* 19.

[16] K. Barth, *ibid.*, 28.

[17] W. Joest, "Gesetz und Evangelium," RGG³ II, 1527.

[18] R. Bring, *Die Erfüllung des Gesetzes durch Christus: Kerygma und Dogma* 5 (1959), I, 11.

[19] R. Bring, *ibid.*

[20] Compare P. Althaus, *Gebot und Gesetz* (Essays for the Promotion of Christian Theology 46/2), Gütersloh, 1952, 7, in reference to W. Elert, G. Ebeling, R. Bring.

[21] W. Joest, *Gesetz und Freiheit*, 71–78.

[22] H. Goldwitzer, *op. cit.*, in positive comment on Karl Barth.

[23] W. Joest, *op. cit.*, 69, in direct connection with Luther.

[24] P. Althaus, *op. cit.*, 33 f.

[25] P. Althaus, *ibid.*, 35.

[26] B. Häring, "Die Stellung des Gesetzes in der Moraltheologie," in V. Redlich, *Moralprobleme im Umbruch der Zeit*, München, 1957, 135.

[27] Compare G. Söhngen, *Gesetz und Evangelium*, München, 1957, and the fundamental article, "Gesetz und Evangelium," in LThK ²IV, 83–835; also *Catholica* XIV (1960)2.

[28] H. Schlier, *Der Brief an die Galater*, Göttingen, ¹¹1951, 200.

[29] R. Schnackenburg, *Die Sitliche Botschaft des Neuen Testamentes*, München, 1954, 138.

[30] Augustine, *De spiritu et littera*, XVII, 29.

[31] Augustine, *ibid.*, XIX, 34.

[32] G. Söhngen, LThK ²IV, 834.

[33] H. Küng, *Rechtfertigung, Die Lehre Karl Barths und eine katholische Bessinung*, Einsiedeln, 1957, 257.

[34] H. Schlier, *Galater*, 200 ff.

[35] B. Häring, *op. cit.*, 142.

[36] H. U. von Balthasar, *Merkmale des Christlichen: Verbum Caro*, Einsiedeln, 1960, 178 f.

[37] B. Häring, *Die Stellung des Gesetzes*, 142.

[38] W. Joest, *Gesetz und Freiheit*, 25.

[39] H. Küng, *op. cit.*

[40] *Ibid.,* 261.

[41] H. U. von Balthasar, *op. cit.*

Chapter 2: PRECEPT AND ORDER OF NATURE

I. *The Validity of the Order of Nature*

[1] Cf. J. Fuchs, *Lex Naturae,* Düsseldorf, 1955, 9 ff.; English edition published by Sheed and Ward, New York, 1965.

[2] E. Brunner, *Der Mensch im Widerspruch,* Zürich, ³1941, 538.

[3] Compare E. Schlink, *Theologie der Lutherischen Bekenntnisschriften,* ²1947, 104 f.; D. Walther, *Kerygma und Dogma* 4(1958), 17–111.

[4] Brunner refers to nature in St. Paul: Rom 1:26; 2:14; 1 Cor 11:14.

[5] E. Brunner, *Gerechtigkeit,* Zürich, 1943, 104 f.

[6] *Ibid.,* 106.

[7] *Ibid.,* 106.

[8] E. Brunner, *Das Gebot und die Ordnungen,* Zurich, 1939, 198.

[9] H. H. Schrey, "Die protestantische Ethik der Gegenwart," in V. Redlich, *Moralprobleme im Umbruch der Zeit,* München, ⁴1957, 51.

[10] W. Künneth, *Theologie der Auferstehung,* München, ⁴1951.

[11] W. Künneth, *Politik zwischen Dämon und Gott,* Berlin, 1954.

[12] H. Thielicke, *Theologische Ethik,* Tübingen, 1955 ff.

[13] J. Fuchs, *op. cit.,* 177.

[14] F. Flückiger, *Geschichte des Naturrechtes,* Zollikon, 1954, I, 287.

[15] K. Rahner, *Wurde und Freiheit des Menschen: Schriften zur Theologie,* Einsiedeln, 1955, II, 256.

II. *The Relation of Norm and Situation*

[1] K. Barth, *Kirchliche Dogmatik* III, 4, Zurich, 1951, 5; hereinafter *KD.*

[2] *KD* III, 4, 9.

[3] E. Brunner, *op. cit.,* 33.

[4] *Ibid.,* 46, citation from Kant: first sentence from the "Foundation for the Metaphysics of Morals." On the meaning of Kant for E. Brunner, confer also his autobiography in *Reformatio,* 11/12/1963.

[5] *Ibid.*, 33.

[6] Citations which follow in the text, with page numbers, all refer to *KD,* III, 4.

[7] A. de Quervain, *Die Heiligung: Ethik,* Zürich, [2]1946, I, 248.

[8] D. Bonhoeffer, *Ethik,* München, 1949, 215.

[9] *ZEE,* 1957/ 1, 6.

[10] Cf. W. Schrage, "Zur formaletischen Deutung der paulinischen Paränese": *Zee,* 1960/4 207–233. In this connection, obviously, material ethics is understood only in an improper sense. Everyone admits that no developed ethics is encountered in the New Testament.

[11] R. Bultmann, *Glauben und Verstehen,* [2]1954, 1, 234.

[12] Cf. H. Preisker, *Das Ethos des Urchristentums,* Gütersloh, [2]1949, 76 f.

[13] W. Schrage, *ZEE,* 1960/4, 208. Following citations in the text are taken from this source.

[14] W. Schrage, see note 12. Cf. also W. Schweizer, "Glaube und Ethos in Neuen und Alten Testament," *ZEE,* 1961/3.

[15] *ZEE,* 1960/4, 245.

[16] Especially in Volume II/1 of his *Theologischen Ethik,* Tübingen, 1955. The marginal numbers are given in the text.

[17] R. Egenter, the article, "Moral Theology," in *LThK,* [2]VII, 614.

[18] R. Schnackenburg, *Die sitliche Botschaft des Neuen Testamentes,* München, 1954, 138.

[19] Cf. W. Trilling, *Das wahre Israel* (Theological Studies, 7), Leipsig, 1959, 169.

[20] See pp. 25 ff.

[21] J. B. Lotz, *Scholastik,* 38 (1963), 336.

[22] Cf. F. Böckle, article "Existential Ethics," in *LThK,* [2]1959, 1301–1304.

Chapter 3: SINNERS AND SIN

[1] E. Kinder, *Die Erbsünde,* Stuttgart, 1959, 40.

[2] *Ibid.*, 82.

[3] *Ibid.*, 56.

[4] Ep. 186 c, n. 16; *Ench.* 27; *De div. quaest. q.* 68, n. 3.

[5] H. Küng, *op. cit,* 178.

[6] J. Regnier, *Der Moderne Mensch und die Sünde,* Würzburg, 1956.

[7] Aquinas, *Summa Theologica,* I. II. 88, 2.

[8] H. Bacht, *Die Welt von Heute und das Gespür für die Sunde: Geist und Leben,* 31 (1958), 9.

[9] "Myth of Sisyphos," in Bacht, *op. cit.*

[10] Aquinas, II. II. 4. 4. ad 3.

[11] W. Joest, *Gesetz und Freiheit,* Göttingen, [2]1956, 58.

[12] E. Schlink, *Gesetz und Evangelium als kontroverstheologisches Problem: Kerygma und Dogma,* 7 (1961), 24.

[13] *WA* XXXIX/1, 542, 5.

[14] *WA* VII. 30, 5 f.

[15] *WA* LVI. 441, 15 f.

[16] Cf. O. Kuss, *Der Romerbrief,* Regensburg, 1959, 462 ff.